Untold Stories of Officer Bob

by

Evan Lipscomb

Copyright 2025 @ Evan Lipscomb
All rights reserved. No part of this publication may be reproduced, distributed or transmitted in any form or by any means, including photocopying, recording, or other electronic or mechanical methods, without the prior written permission of the copyright owner.
This is a work of fiction. Names, characters, places, and incidents are the product of the author's imagination.

Edited by Kevin Davis
Published by Kevisyde Entertainment
ISBN: 979-8-90046-832-7 (Paperback)
ISBN: 978-1-257-07009-1 (Hardcover)

Chapter 1: The Empty House Standoff

The night air hung heavy, damp with summer's fading warmth. Officer Bob eased his cruiser down Elm Street, headlights cutting swaths of yellow through the gathering darkness. He ran a hand over the worn leather of his radio mic, the familiar weight grounding him. Tonight was like any other—until the dispatch call crackled over:

> "Units 14, 16, 18—shots fired at 342 Maple. Approach with caution."

Bob's pulse quickened. He checked his mirrors, then switched on the siren. The engine growled as he accelerated, the neighborhood's peaceful veneer shattered by echoing gunfire. He slid on gloves, recalling his first academy lesson: "Always expect the unexpected."

Within moments, Bob arrived behind Officer John's cruiser, its lights already spinning red and blue. Officer Lynn stood forward, scanning the house. Through the haze of the siren's glow, Bob heard the steady cricket-song of the lawn, untouched hedges trembling in the breeze.

He stepped out, boots on the warm asphalt, and fell into formation. John moved left toward the ivy-clad garage while Lynn and Bob fanned out to the front porch. Bob's fingers traced the grooves of his service belt—baton, cuffs, flashlight—reminders of his duty.

"Clear this flank," John whispered, voice low over the radio. Bob tipped his head. In that instant, time seemed to slow: the hum of cicadas, a neighbor's distant dog barking, his own breath in the humid air.

Bob pressed against the side of the house, flashlight ready. The wood siding felt cool under his palm. He crept forward, eyes peeled for movement. Every sense sharpened—until John's calm voice broke the tension: "Bob, this side's clear."

Bob exhaled, the knot in his chest easing. He tapped Lynn's shoulder; they exchanged a nod and advanced toward the front door, unaware that the real danger waited just beyond the threshold.

Bob's flashlight beam quivered as he and Lynn crouched low at the threshold. The door's faded white paint curled at the edges, decades of neglect visible in each crack. Bob pressed his gloved hand to the frame, listening. Somewhere deep inside, his heartbeat pounded like a warning drum.

"Ready?" he whispered to Lynn. She nodded, eyes wide but determined. Bob slid the door ajar, the hinges protesting with a high-pitched squeal that seemed deafening in the hush. He froze, every muscle coiled.

On the other side, moonlight filtered through a cracked window, casting ghostly patterns on the carpet. Dust motes danced in the beam. Bob inched forward, his flashlight tracing corners where shadows pooled.

Lynn swept her light over overturned furniture: a toppled chair, a broken vase, shards of porcelain scattered like fallen stars. Each clue tightened the coil of suspense.

When they reached the bedroom closet, Bob paused. His mind flashed back to his first case—how fear could paralyze if you let it—and he forced himself to breathe slowly.

"On three," he murmured. "One… two… three."

He yanked the closet door open, body tense like a cat ready to pounce. Lynn swung in beside him. A single floorboard creaked behind them and Bob whirled as Lynn's shout cut the silence:

"There's someone in the closet!"

Bob and John froze for a heartbeat before Bob barked, "Stand back, Lynn!" His voice was sharp, slicing through the tension like a blade. He planted himself at the edge of the doorway, flashlight in one hand, radio clipped to his belt vibrating with distant dispatch updates.

John swallowed and looked at Bob. "You sure about this?" he whispered, voice taut.

Bob pressed a firm hand to John's shoulder. "You open the door. I'll cover you. Got it?"

John exhaled, steeled his nerves, and nodded. With careful precision, he reached for the doorknob. Bob shined his light inside the closet, revealing a narrow space lined with coats and boxes—perfect for a hidden assailant.

John eased the door open an inch. A brass barrel glinted from the darkness.

Bob's heart thundered in his ears. "Close it! Close it now!" he ordered. John slammed the door shut with all his might, the wood shuddering on its hinges.

Lynn backed up, breath caught. Bob pivoted, mind racing. "Smoke grenades," he muttered, radioing John's pack. "We need smoke grenades—lure him out." CT

John's voice crackled back: "Roger that. Heading for the vest." He retreated to the staging area.

Bob stayed by the door, eyes locked on the closet. Seconds stretched like hours. Every nerve in his body screamed for action.

Then, from behind a broken side window, Bob spotted movement—a flash of jacket. He peered through the glass. "It's clear—he's alone," he whispered over the radio.

Moments later, John returned, tugging at the pack. Bob grabbed two smoke canisters, his grip steady. He sealed his flashlight and cracked a grenade open, breathing deep. "On three," Bob warned. "One… two… three." He shoved the first canister under the door with a smooth arc, then sprinted outside to cover the window.

Through the smoke-shrouded doorway, Bob watched as a shape emerged, coughing and disoriented. The opaque haze clawed at his eyes, turning the closet into a ghostly void. Bob's fingers itched at his holster, every instinct screaming to act.

Lynn and John pressed close, weapons raised. A silhouette stumbled, then dropped the gun with a clatter that rang through the mist.

Bob stepped forward. "Drop everything and put your hands where I can see them!" His voice boomed, cutting through the smoky air.

The figure obeyed, coughs echoing off the closet walls. Bob waded in, flashlight slicing through the grey veil to reveal the gunman's terrified eyes.

Minutes later, breathing heavy, Bob cuffed the surrendering suspect and guided him outside, where fresh air hit like a wave. Dispatch arrived moments after, securing the scene.

Bob wiped soot from his uniform and settled onto the tailgate of his cruiser, only the glow of his flashlight to keep company. He retrieved a small leather-bound notebook—his unofficial journal—and flipped to a blank page. The night's adrenaline had thinned his thoughts to raw wires, and he needed to unspool them.

June 12, 11:27 PM
House on Maple. Gunshots. Smoke. I've never felt heat like that grenade blast—my face stung even through the mask. John's hand shook when he closed the closet door; Lynn's shout still echoes in my ears. At that moment, I saw the gunman's eyes—wide, terrified, human. Bob paused, letting memory settle. He stared at the lines forming beneath his pen.

Reflections:
Fear can freeze you. Last night, I remembered why we train—so instinct takes over. I trusted John to open the door; he trusted me to watch his back. That trust is our real shield. He tapped the notebook, considering the discord of quiet that followed violence.

Lessons Learned:

1. Always check every exit—windows lie.
2. Never underestimate the power of a well-timed distraction.
3. After the smoke cleared, I felt more anger at the waste of life than relief at the arrest. Why do we keep doing this? Because someone has to.

The pages glowed under his pen's scratch as he wrote his final thought.

Closing Thought:
Tonight, I saved a life by ending another's threat. The badge demands compromise, but I'll keep walking this line—learning, protecting, living.

He snapped the notebook shut and leaned back, watching the afterimage of the gas canister dissolve into the night air. Tomorrow would bring paperwork and debriefs; tonight he let the words speak what words otherwise couldn't.

Chapter 2: The Fedora Bandit

Bob rolled into the warehouse district under a slate-gray sky, the hum of rain-soaked pavement humming beneath his tires. Droplets raced down the windshield as he eased his cruiser into a shadowed loading bay. He glanced at his watch—3:42 PM sharp.

Exiting the vehicle, Bob clicked off his wipers and inhaled the scent of damp wood and fresh leather. Boxes stamped "Hats Only" towered in neat rows, punctuated by pools of pale security-light glow. Some lamps flickered erratically; others were dark—ideal blind spots for a thief.

He grabbed his flashlight and radio, patting his belt to ensure his baton and cuffs were secure. Each step splashed shallow puddles underfoot, echoing faintly against concrete walls. Bob's breath fogged in the cold air, mixing with the mist rising off the ground.

Approaching the nearest stack of crates, he moved deliberately, sensing alert. The rain's patter on metal roofs played a steady rhythm, masking smaller noises. Bob's eyes darted among the shadows, searching for any sign of movement.

A sudden clang—metal on metal—snapped his gaze to a narrow gap between two pallets. He froze, body taut. The faintest silhouette flitted across the gap, disappearing behind a crate.

Bob raised his flashlight and swept its beam side to side, illuminating rows of stacked boxes. His pulse quickened; Fedora Man was close.

He called softly into his radio: "Team, this is Bob. I have a visual on a suspect between crates five and six. Proceed with caution."

Silence answered, then a crackle: "Copy that. Units moving in."

Bob crouched, edging forward along the crate line. Each breath felt amplified, each heartbeat a drumroll. He tightened his grip on the flashlight, ready for whatever lurked in the shadows.

Bob rounded the corner of crate row five, heart hammering as his light bobbed across stacked boxes. There—partially obscured behind a tall crate—stood a slim figure clad in dark clothing and, unmistakably, a black fedora pulled low over their eyes. Fedora Man's gloved hand hovered just above a crate labeled "Premium Felt Collection."

Bob raised his voice, firm and controlled. "Freeze! Hands where I can see them!" His radio crackled: "Bob to Team, suspect in sight."

The thief spun, drawing a sleek fedora from the crate. With a swift motion, he flung the hat skyward, as if taunting Bob. It landed atop a nearby barrel, its shadow dancing in the swivel light.

Bob advanced slowly, covering every step. "Step away from the merchandise. You're under arrest." His badge glinted silver in the beam.

Fedora Man let out a low chuckle, tilting his head. "Arrest me? For hats?" He waved a stack of fedoras—crimson, navy, striped—in front of him. "These beauties are worth more than your cruiser."

Bob's jaw tightened. "My badge isn't for sale. Drop the hats and get on the ground."

The bandit hesitated, eyes flicking between the crate and Bob's unwavering stance. Rain slid off his hat's brim, tracing lines across the leather band.

In one fluid motion, Bob drew his cuffs. "Last warning."

A tense beat. Then, with a sigh, Fedora Man let the hats spill to the floor like fallen petals. He raised his hands. "Alright, officer. You win."

Bob stepped forward, snapping cuff links into place. He secured the bandit's wrists. "Let's go."

Two backup officers emerged from the shadows, nodding in approval as they approached to take custody. Fedora Man tipped his hat—an ironic salute—before being led away.

Bob gave a curt nod to the arriving officers. "Search him and secure the merchandise." He knelt by the fallen hats, lifting each brim gently before handing them to a waiting sergeant.

"Looks like thirteen in total, sir," the sergeant reported, counting neatly in the dim warehouse glow.

Bob clicked open his evidence bag and placed the hats one by one inside, careful not to crease the felt. Fedora Man muttered under his breath through damp curls of rain, but Bob ignored the protests.

Once the evidence was secured, Bob stood and patted the thief's shoulder—firm but not unkind. "Don't make this habit," he said, voice low. Fedora Man cracked a sardonic grin but said nothing.

Bob retrieved his radio. "Command, this is Bob. Suspect in custody, stolen goods secured. Requesting transport and a unit to catalog evidence."

"Copy that, Bob," came the reply. "ETA back at station in ten."

He watched as the officers led the bandit toward an armored van, crates of hats in tow. The gentle patter of rain drummed on the roof as Bob surveyed the scene, satisfaction mixing with the steady hum of duty.

Before leaving, Bob took one last look at the stacked crates. The warehouse was silent once more, save for dripping water and Bob's measured breath.

He slid back into his cruiser, the warmth of the cab a sharp contrast to the cold exterior night. On the drive back, Bob reviewed the case in his mind—every move, every decision—mentally logging notes for his report.

Bob eased into his cruiser, the heater humming to life as he settled the wheel. The warehouse lights receded in his rearview mirror, replaced by the blurred streaks of streetlamps on rain-slick asphalt. He pressed the radio button. "Bob to HQ—case closed, heading back now."

Silence, then the familiar crackle: "Copy that, Bob. Good work."

He exhaled slowly, tracing the lines of his notebook in his mind—every move cataloged, every decision weighed. The absurdity of a hat thief still lingered at the edges of his thoughts, coaxing a wry smile.

He reached into the glove box and pulled out a bar of chocolate—the same one he kept for late-night stakeouts. Unwrapping it, he savored a bite, the sweetness cutting through the damp chill. "Even hat thieves deserve a taste of irony," he murmured to himself.

The city skyline loomed ahead, neon signs flickering in puddles. Bob flicked his blinkers and turned onto Main Street. His mind drifted to the next report—a missing person, overdue welfare check. Duty never slept.

He parked under the fluorescent glow of the precinct's entrance, rain trickling down his windshield. As he stepped out, he felt the weight of the day's oddities—crime and comedy intertwined in Fedora Man's spree.

Inside, the station was alive with chatter—officers finishing paperwork, dispatch calls chiming. Bob nodded to familiar faces, his uniform still damp but his resolve dry and steady.

He placed the evidence bag on his desk and set the stolen hats neatly beside the computer. As he logged into the system, he paused, watching their felt peaks and brims cast shadows on the desk.

In that moment, Bob realized: every case, no matter how small, carried its own story. And whether chasing down armed gunmen or cunning hat thieves, he was there—telling those stories one page at a time.

Bob exhaled, placing his badge back onto his uniform before retrieving his notebook and pen. With the warehouse behind him, he found a quiet corner under an awning, jotting down observations:

Case Notes:
"Fedora Man" was cornered after a precise tip—likely from a disgruntled ex-employee. Stolen hats recovered: 13. Unusual MO: targets high-end vintage fedoras.

Tapping his pen, Bob reflected:

Thoughts:
The whimsical nature of this thief belies a pattern—value-driven, almost theatrical. There's a showmanship here I can't ignore.

He paused, watching the rain trace paths down the awning's edge.

Next Steps:

1. Interview local vintage shops for similar thefts.
2. Check secondhand marketplace for suspicious listings.
3. Follow up on the tipster—know who provided the intel.

Notebook closed, Bob slid it into his coat pocket. He gave the awning one last glance before striding back to his cruiser, the ticking of the rain matching his resolve. Dawn broke with a weak sun, mist still clinging to the sidewalk as Bob returned to the station. He swapped his soaked coat for a fresh one and grabbed a coffee from the roll-call kettle. His notebook lay open: "Interview vintage shop owners—0900."

He tapped the timestamp. At 8:45 AM, Bob sat in his cruiser outside "Madeline's Millinery," a quaint shop with lace curtains and a polished mahogany sign. He sipped his coffee, eyes on the door. The bell jingled at precisely 9:01 as Madeline herself emerged, dusting her hat display. Bob approached, badge visible. "Morning, Ms. Hart. Mind if I come in?" Madeline offered a polite nod. "Officer Bob. Please—do come in." Inside, rows of fedoras and cloches lined velvet shelves. The air smelled of lemon polish and wool.

Bob gestured to a chair. "I'm here about the recent thefts. Have you noticed anything odd—missing hats, new customers asking questions?" Her face tightened. "First the warehouse shipment, now my shop. Yesterday, a tall man in a black fedora browsed for nearly twenty minutes before leaving empty-handed."

Bob flipped to a fresh page in his notebook. "Can you describe him?" Madeline hesitated, then spoke: "He had a certain flair—tilted his hat just so. Didn't look like a thief—more like a connoisseur."

She tapped a finger on her lip. "He asked about the history of one particular hat, then departed through the back door." Bob's mind clicked. "Did you get a license plate or see which way he went?"

Madeline shook her head. "I thought it best not to get too close." Bob stood, sliding his notebook into his coat. "Thank you, Ms. Hart. I'll follow up on the back alley exit." As he stepped outside, he noted the narrow lane to his left, lined with dumpsters and flickering alley lights.

He walked briskly to the alley, scanning dumpsters for footprints or discarded items. A torn scrap of fabric caught his eye—black wool, matching the stolen hats' segments. He bagged it, satisfaction warming him more than the morning light.

Bob unfolded the scrap of black wool beneath the flickering alley light, pressing it against his glove to confirm the texture: supple, vintage-grade felt. He tucked it into an evidence bag and dialed dispatch. "Bob to HQ—evidence collected, heading to the secondhand market on Jefferson."

The marketplace sprawled under a canopy of tarps, vendors packing away goods as dawn crept over rooftops. Bob navigated between folding tables strewn with leather jackets and old vinyl records. His eyes scanned hastily scrawled signs: "Fedoras & More," "Vintage Hats—Cheap."

Near a rickety booth, a stack of fedoras caught his gaze—one bore the same distinctive seam as the warehouse's missing hats. Bob approached, pulling on latex gloves. He lifted the hat and compared it to photos in his notebook. Match confirmed.

"Morning," he said to the vendor, who blinked in surprise. "I'm Officer Bob. I need to catalog those hats as evidence." The vendor's eyes darted around. "Uh, sure, officer. They're—uh—just old stock." He tried to slide the stack away.

Bob set a boot on the table to block him. "I'm holding them until forensics clears it. Who sold them to you?" The vendor swallowed. "Look, I just buy and sell. Some guy in a black hat left them here last night. Paid cash." Bob's mind raced. "Cash amount?" "Two hundred each," the vendor stammered. "He said he was a collector."

Bob snapped cufflinks into place. "Right. You're a key witness. I'll need your statement. Also, I want any security footage you have."

The vendor nodded, defeated. Bob bagged the hats one by one and tagged them. He stepped back into the drizzle of morning light, evidence in hand, puzzle pieces aligning.

Bob tapped his finger against the notebook where he'd scribbled "Follow payment trail: Jefferson Market." He opened the precinct's database on his laptop, entering each cash amount—two hundred, two hundred, two hundred—searching for recent ATM withdrawals or large currency exchanges. A pattern emerged: deposits at the same downtown credit union, just blocks from the old train depot.

He grabbed his coat and cruiser keys. "Time to set a trap," he muttered, sliding into his car.

By evening, Bob parked near the deserted depot, its steel beams humming with the echo of distant trains. He positioned himself behind rusted freight cars, camera and flashlight at the ready. He placed a single vintage hat on a wooden crate—bait irresistible to Fedora Man.

Minutes crawled by. Then, a silent figure slipped from the shadows, fedora tipped low. The bandit's eyes lit at the sight of the hat. He crept forward, gloved fingers brushing the brim—just as Bob flicked on a spotlight. "Hold it right there!" Bob called. Fedora Man froze, eyes narrowing. Backup cars' lights whirled in, sealing exit routes. The thief looked around, calculating.

Bob advanced, voice steady. "Drop that hat and step away." After a tense pause, the bandit raised his hands, raising the chosen fedora in surrender. Under the depot lights, his face looked weary rather than defiant. Bob cuffed him quickly. "You won't be collecting any more hats."

Bob's phone buzzed—a message from dispatch: "Data from credit union confirms deposits. The suspect will collect the next shipment at 24th Street dock at 8 PM." He smiled, the puzzle nearly complete. As dusk settled, Bob cruised to the aging docks, the river's lull echoing against rusted cranes. He positioned backup teams at key exits and called them in quietly: "Eyes on gangway, north and south. I'm going in."

Clad in plain clothes and a reflective vest, Bob waded through stacked pallets, the smell of brine mixing with diesel. He spotted a lone figure at the far end, methodically unpacking crates. Fedora Man's hat sat atop a wooden spool like a crown.

Bob approached slowly, badge discreetly in hand. "Pretty night for business," he quipped. The thief looked up, surprise flickering in his eyes. Without hesitation, Bob sprang the trap: two officers emerged from behind containers, blocking the suspect. The bandit's face was drained of color.

"Game's up," Bob said, stepping forward. Fedora Man's shoulders slumped in defeat. Handcuffs clicked shut. Bob patted his shoulder. "No more midnight collections, okay?"

Backup agents swept in, securing the final crates and escorting the bandit away. Bob stood on the dock, the river's moonlit reflection shimmering at his feet. Bob returned to the precinct under a clearing sky, the early hours lending a hush to the normally bustling station. He stepped through the door, shedding his vest and badge like an old coat, then made his way to the briefing room.

Inside, a half-dozen officers gathered around a long table strewn with case files. Lieutenant Ramirez looked up, exhaustion and pride in equal measure. "Good work, Bob. Fedora Man's off the streets for good."

Bob nodded and set his notebook and the final evidence bag on the table. "All recovered hats are accounted for—sixty-two total across all sites." He tapped his pen. "I'll upload statements and footage to the server tonight."

Ramirez offered a weary smile. "Still can't believe hats were the big score. But every case matters. You handled it well." Bob allowed himself a small grin. "Even the quirky ones." The lieutenant stood and stretched. "Get some rest. We'll need you sharp on the Maple Street report tomorrow."

Bob gathered his gear and headed for the locker room. He paused by the wall-mounted phone and dialed home. "Hey, it's me. Case closed—hats are in the evidence room. I'll see you at breakfast."

He slipped on his coat and stepped back into the night air, lights of the station receding behind him. As he drove home, he reflected on the strange duality of his job—moments of high adrenaline followed by the mundane paperwork and phone calls.

Arriving at his front porch, Bob turned off the cruiser and inhaled the faint scent of dawn creeping in. He looked at the badge on his dashboard and whispered, "Another story told."

Chapter 3: The Gruesome Streets

Dawn's pale light broke through low-hanging clouds as Officer Bob and John's cruiser screeched to a halt outside 118 Oak Avenue. The street was silent except for the muted drip of rain from rooftiles and the distant wail of a siren. Bob's stomach tightened—murder in broad daylight was a rarity in their quiet town.

He climbed from the vehicle, boots crunching on wet asphalt, and pulled on his coat collar against the chill. John joined him, notebook open, eyes scanning the small crowd gathered behind yellow tape. Neighbors peered from doorways, their faces etched with shock.

Bob touched the tape's edge. "Keep a perimeter," he instructed a rookie officer. Then, voice low to John: "Let's approach—slow and steady." They weaved between uniformed officers and curious onlookers, boots splashing through shallow puddles.

As they neared the front lawn, the starkest sight met them: the victim, a young woman, lay face-down on the damp grass, crimson blooming against the green. Her phone lay cracked beside her hand, raindrops pooling on its screen.

Bob knelt, careful not to disturb evidence. The air smelled sharply of iron and rain-washed earth. He reached for latex gloves and donned them, gaze steady as he scanned for wounds: a single, precise stab wound just below the shoulder blade.

John's voice cut softly: "Witnesses say they saw someone run east on Oak. Dark coat—hood up." He flipped through his notebook, scribbling furiously.

Bob studied the body's position, noting footprints in the soft soil: one set leading from the street, another disappearing toward the hedgerow. He traced the path with his finger. "Let's follow those prints," he said, rising with resolve.

Behind them, paramedics tended to neighbors in mild shock as Bob and John slipped past the tape into the hedgerow, ready to trace the killer's path. Bob and John crept through the hedgerow, where muddy footprints pressed deep into the damp earth. Bob crouched to examine them—size twelve, heel-first, then toe—a hurried stride betrayed by errant clumps of soil. He traced the line eastward, John illuminating the path with his flashlight.

The footprints led them into the backyard of the adjacent property, where a wrought-iron gate lay ajar. Bob pushed it open, the hinges squealing in protest. Beyond, a narrow alley framed by tall fences opened onto a deserted side street. John shone his light along the pavement. "Only tracks and rain puddles—no sign of a vehicle."

Bob nodded. "Chances are he ran off on foot until he could ditch the coat." He patted his coat pocket. "Let's check for any blood or dropped items." They followed the trail past a fallen trash can and behind a row of overgrown hedges until Bob spotted a dark smudge—fresh blood—on a discarded scrap of cardboard. He bagged it carefully. "Good find," John murmured. "This could be our break." Bob radioed in: "Evidence collected. Following the footpath to the alley. Requesting a K-9 unit."

A distant bark answered. Moments later, Scout, the department's German Shepherd, bounded toward them, nose low. Bob attached the lead. "Let's see where Scout takes us." Scout sniffed the ground, then bolted down the alley. Bob and John sprinted after, adrenaline surging as the dog led them toward the next clue. Scout veered left at a pile of discarded boxes, pausing at a narrow gap between fences. Bob and John pressed close, scanning for movement.

Through the sliver of space, they spotted a weathered shed door, its hinges rusted and paint peeling. John motioned. "Could be a hideout." Bob clicked on his flashlight, beam cutting through dusty air as he nudged the door open with his baton. Inside, the shed was cramped—garden tools, broken lawn chairs, and a tarp-covered object in the corner.

Bob approached slowly, hand near his holster. He yanked the tarp back, revealing a bloodstained hoodie and a small knife with a wooden handle. John knelt beside the items. "Looks fresh."

Bob bagged the evidence. "This is what we needed." He radioed dispatch: "Bob to HQ—found suspect's gear in shed on 120 Oak. Sending K-9 on standby for scent confirmation." Scout sniffed at the hoodie and growled softly, tail wagging in focused rhythm. Bob nodded, satisfied. "Good job, Scout."

As they exited the shed, Bob felt the weight of the case settle in. They had a motive, weapon, and a scent trail. Now it was a matter of closing the loop.Bob stepped out of the shed into the muted morning light, the weight of the hoodie and knife evidence heavy in his pack. He glanced at John. "We've got him cornered. Time to track the scent."

Scout strained at the leash, nose to the ground, leading them back toward Oak Avenue. Bob followed, careful to step where John hadn't, preserving the trail. Every few yards, Scout paused—then forged on, dragging them down a side street lined with row houses.

They emerged onto Maple Street, where the air smelled faintly of freshly baked bread and damp concrete. Scout pulled them to a stoop where a man in a dark hoodie sat, staring at his feet. Bob raised his voice. "Sir, get up—hands where I can see them!" The man bolted, hoodie slipping off in the scuffle to reveal a shock of dark hair and panicked eyes. Bob lunged, catching him by the arm as John cuffed him from behind. The man's breath came in ragged gasps.

Bob patted the suspect down, retrieving a knife's sheath from the back pocket. "Convenient timing," he said as John lifted the hood from the pavement and matched it to the bagged evidence. Nearby, neighbors peeked from windows. Bob called over his shoulder, "Please stay inside—we're fine." Then, to the suspect, "You have the right to remain silent…"

With the cuffs secure, Bob radioed it in. "Suspect in custody, Maple and Oak. Evidence matched—clothing and weapon recovered. Sending K-9 back to the station." He exhaled, scanning the quiet street. "Good work, Scout." The dog wagged and licked Bob's hand, ready for the next step: transport and interrogation.

Bob and John escorted the suspect to their squad car, Scout padding alongside. The man's shoulders sagged, the reality of capture settling in. Rain began again, misting in the streetlight glow. Bob opened the passenger door. "Get in. Hands on the dash." Once they secured him inside, Bob climbed into the driver's seat, voice soft but firm. "Your name?"

The suspect stared straight ahead. "M-Marcus Hale." John knocked lightly on the window. "Marcus, do you know why we found your hoodie and knife in that shed?" Marcus swallowed. "I panicked. I didn't mean to… she came at me—I was scared." His voice trembled.

Bob exchanged a look with John. "The victim said she barely saw you. One stab wound—clean. You planned this." Marcus shook his head, tears mixing with rain on his face. "I didn't plan a murder. It just… happened."

Bob's jaw tightened. "We'll let the evidence speak. Why'd you run?" "Because I knew I'd go back to jail." His shoulders collapsed. "I lost control." Bob reached into his coat pocket and pulled out his notebook. "Okay. We'll sort it all at the station. For now, you're coming with us."

He closed the cruiser door, and the three of them—Bob, John, and the suspect—headed back toward headquarters as Scout trotted at the side, ears perked and ready for the next step. Forensic reports pinged in just after lunch: the blood on the knife, hoodie, and scrap of cardboard all matched the victim's DNA. Bob studied the printout, relief and resolve mingling in his chest. It was time to finalize charges.

He met John in the bullpen. "Everything's confirmed. Marcus will be charged with second-degree murder, and we've got the premeditation pinned by that weapon and the path he took." John nodded. "Let's wrap up the warrant returns and transport him to the county lockup."

By mid-afternoon, Bob walked into the holding area. Marcus sat on the bench, shoulders slumped. Bob read aloud the formal charge sheet, then signed it, pressing a copy into the suspect's hands. "You have the right to an attorney," he said, voice firm but compassionate.

With that, Marcus was escorted out. The tension in Bob's shoulders eased—a rare case completely tied up. Back at his desk, Bob typed his final case notes, summarizing the investigation from the crime scene through the shed, the apartment search, and the forensic confirmation. He added a final reflection:

> *"Every step—from the first footprint to the lab results—reminded me that even the smallest clue can break a case wide open. Justice is a mosaic built one piece at a time."*

He saved the file and closed his laptop. Outside, afternoon sun filtered through the blinds. Tomorrow brought new calls, new stories—but for now, this one was done. Later that evening, Bob stood outside Marcus's apartment, warrant in hand. The building loomed silent under streetlights, its narrow windows dark. He knocked firmly and announced, "Police—search warrant for room 3B."

A nervous clerk buzzed him in. Bob and John navigated the dim hallway to the door. Bob's flashlight beam cut through stale air as he turned the lock. Inside, the apartment felt cramped—cloth jackets draped over chairs, a small desk littered with papers.

John secured the perimeter while Bob swept the room. On the desk lay a photograph of the victim pinned with a ribbon, surrounded by hastily scribbled notes mapping Oak Avenue. Bob carefully bagged the photo and notes, recognizing them as crucial evidence.

He moved to the bedroom closet and froze. The door creaked as he nudged it open, revealing more blood-splattered clothing. His stomach tightened. Methodically, he collected the garments—each a mute confession. John called softly, "Got everything?" Bob exhaled and nodded. "Let's go."

Back in the hallway, Scout's keen nose verified the scent trail as they retraced their steps out. Bob closed the door behind him, the echo lingering like a shuttered memory. On the drive back to headquarters, Bob stared ahead while John reviewed the collected items. Every piece—photo, notes, hoodie, knife, clothing—wove together the narrative of what happened. Bob knew this chapter of the case was closing, but the story of that life lost would stay with him always.

The next morning, Bob returned to his desk with a fresh cup of coffee and the assembled evidence arrayed before him: photos, notes, clothing swatches, and the bloodstained knife. He replayed the case in his mind, tracing each step until the outline was as clear as dawn light. He opened his report and began typing:

> **Incident Report #2025-0312**
> **Location:** 118 Oak Avenue
> **Victim:** Jane Reynolds, female, 28
> **Suspect:** Marcus Hale, male, 32

He summarized the discovery of footprints, Scout's trail to the shed, the arrest on Maple Street, and the search of 3B. Each bullet point felt like a stitch binding the story together. As he drafted the "Detective's Narrative" section, he paused at his reflection:

> *"I still remember my first homicide call—hands trembled, stomach churned. But today, every procedure felt instinctive. That confidence comes from every case like this."*

He attached digital copies of the forensic reports, then saved and submitted the full file. A chime signaled the printer: two hard copies spit out.

He tucked one into his case folder, handed the other to John for the lieutenant's review. Leaning back, Bob allowed himself a moment's relief. Justice had been served, and the community could heal. But the weight of that life—Jane's life—remained heavy. He closed his eyes and whispered a silent vow: to keep telling these stories faithfully, one page at a time. Bob glanced at the clock on his desk—4:15 PM—then stood and stretched.

He grabbed his coat and headed back out, intent on one last task: visiting the victim's family to deliver condolences and ensure they understood the progress of the case. He exited the precinct and drove to the Reynolds residence, a tidy home with a flower-lined path. The door opened before he could knock, revealing Mrs. Reynolds, her face drawn with grief. "Officer Bob," she managed softly, ushering him inside. The living room was hushed, photos of Jane smiling on every surface. Bob settled in and spoke with gentle clarity. "I'm so sorry for your loss," he began. "We've arrested the suspect, and the evidence is strong. I wanted you to hear that from me directly."

Mrs. Reynolds nodded, tears welling. "Thank you. It means a great deal to know you've done everything possible." Bob handed her a printed timeline of events, explaining each step: the initial report, evidence collection, arrest, and charge filing. With each detail, he saw relief mingle with sorrow in her eyes. After a respectful pause, he offered, "If you have any questions or need anything—support services, updates—please call me anytime."

She took a shaky breath and managed a small smile. "Thank you, Officer Bob. For everything." Bob rose, placing a hand on her shoulder. "Take care of yourself." He left quietly, closing the door with reverence.

Back in his cruiser, Bob exhaled deeply. He knew justice might bring closure, but healing would take time—for the family and for himself. He started the engine and headed home, the sun dipping low as pages turned on another chapter of his life's work.

Bob returned to the precinct under soft twilight, the station's fluorescent lights greeting him like a beacon. He hung his coat and retrieved his notebook once more. On the final page for this case, he wrote:

> **Closing Reflection:**
> *Jane Reynolds deserved answers and justice. We delivered both. But behind every file number is a person—a daughter, a friend, a dreamer. I carry their stories with me.*

He snapped the notebook shut and placed it alongside the printed report. Turning off his desk lamp, he paused at the doorway and glanced back at the evidence board—photos, printouts, and Scout's tracking map still pinned in place.

With a final nod, he flicked the switch, and the board went dark. Another case closed, another chapter written. As he stepped into the night, he carried with him the weight of his promise: to protect, to serve, and to tell the untold stories that needed hearing.

Chapter 4: Pool Shark Showdown

On a rare Friday night off, the neon glow of Joe's Diner sign beckoned Officer Bob for his usual burger and coffee. The parking lot buzzed with energy from the adjoining pool hall—shouts, racking balls, the dulled thwack of strikes. Tonight, Bob would trade his badge for a cue stick, and discover that sometimes life's greatest cases are solved one pocket at a time.

The neon sign above Joe's Diner flickered in soft blues and reds, casting long shadows across the parking lot. Bob cut the engine of his cruiser and stretched, grateful for a night off. His uniform still hung beneath his coat, but for now, he was simply a hungry man craving a burger and a break from the past week's chaos.

He pushed open the diner door to the familiar clink of chrome and the warm hiss of the grill. "Evening, Lou," he greeted the cook, who flipped a spatula with practiced ease. "Burger and coffee, please." "Coming right up," Lou replied, sliding a fresh bun onto the grill. Behind Bob, the pool hall's muffled cacophony of shouts and ricochets seeped through the shared wall.

Bob sipped his coffee and watched a group of teens pour in, cue sticks in hand. One of them—a lanky kid in a backwards cap—shot Bob a respectful nod. Bob returned the gesture with a half-smile: he'd broken up more than one under-age game in his time.

When Lou set a steaming burger on the counter, Bob inhaled the savory scent. He paid, then picked up his prize. As he turned to leave, the diner door burst open and two young men, faces flushed with adrenaline, tumbled out into the lot arguing. "You double-crossed me on that eight ball!" one yelled, shoving the other. Bob stepped forward, badge half-visible beneath his coat. "Hey, take it easy—you're on private property."

The first kid squared up. "Mind your business, officer." Bob kept his tone calm. "My business is keeping the peace. Now cool off or I'll have to ask you both to come inside." They glared, fists clenched. Bob noticed one reaching for something in his pocket—too quick. Instinct took over: Bob lunged, wrapping an arm around the kid's shoulder, pinning him against the car door. The second boy froze, eyes wide. "Hands out where I can see them," Bob ordered. "Both of you."

The frozen moment stretched as the diner lights glinted off Bob's badge. The teens slowly lowered their hands, tension draining from their shoulders. Bob released his hold. "Sit tight. I'll get Lou to hold your coats while I figure this out." As he guided them back inside, Bob realized: sometimes the line between off-duty and on-duty blurred in unexpected ways—especially when a pool hall showdown turned personal.

Bob escorted the two teens back inside Joe's Diner and directed them to a corner booth. Lou hovered behind the counter, arms crossed, watching the scene. Bob kept his voice low. "Name and age," he said to the first boy, the one in the cap. "Jake—Jake Tanner," the teen muttered. "Seventeen." Bob nodded, then turned to the second. "You?" "Eric Malone," the other replied, voice trembling. "Eighteen." Bob glanced at Lou. "Keep an eye on these two, will ya? I'll be right back."

He stepped into the pool hall and approached the table where bikes had been racked. Cue balls lay scattered, the felt stained from too many high-stakes games. He scanned the players, then crossed to a grizzled middle-aged man polishing a stick. "Evening, Sam," Bob said.

Sam looked up, eyebrows raised. "Officer," Sam replied. "What brings you here tonight?" Bob gestured toward the teens in the diner. "These two were causing a scene. Thought I'd check if there's more to their argument."

Sam leaned on his cue. "Jake's been itching for a bankroll game. Eric stiffed him on a bet, said he'd pay up after his shift." Bob frowned. "Underage gambling?" Sam shrugged. "Just some extra cash. Nothing violent. They come here every Friday."

Bob exhaled. "Alright. No violence, no weapons—just a bad bet. I'm going to issue a warning. But any more trouble, and it gets official." Sam nodded. "Understood." Bob returned to the diner, where Lou had already fetched clipboard and pen. He wrote out a citation warning about trespassing and disorderly conduct, then handed it to Jake. "Sign here," he said, pointing. Jake scrawled his name, shoulders slumping in relief. Eric did the same. Bob folded the warnings. "Next time, settle your scores on the table, not the pavement." Both teens nodded. Bob gave them a firm but encouraging look. "You're free to go—just keep it clean."

They exited together, more as uneasy allies than adversaries. Bob watched them disappear into the night, then turned back to Lou. "Thanks for holding down the fort," he said, collecting his burger. Lou grinned. "Anytime. You sure know how to make a night interesting." Bob shrugged with a half-smile. "Just part of the job—even on my night off."

He took a hearty bite of his burger, savoring the familiar taste as the pool-ball clacks echoed in the next room. Bob lingered in the diner doorway, watching the teens head off before turning back toward the pool hall. The familiar clack of balls and low murmur of voices beckoned him. He took his burger to a small round table by the window, unfolded the wrapper, and settled in for a bite, eyes still on the pool room's entrance.

A waitress, Marcy, slid over with a fresh cup of coffee. "On the house," she whispered. "You've earned it." Bob nodded gratefully and took a sip. The warmth spread through him. Behind him, the diner's seated patrons returned to their meals, but Bob's attention remained split between the comfort of his burger and the pool hall's activity.

Finishing his first bite, he rose and pushed through the swinging door into the smoky atmosphere. At the far end, the lanky kid from earlier—Jake—had joined a group of regulars around a table marked "Bankroll Only." Their whispered wagers floated on the air. Bob cleared his throat. "Mind if I join?" he asked. Heads turned. Sam the owner nodded. "Help yourself, officer."

Bob slipped in, pulling out a stool. The players eyed him with a mix of curiosity and respect. One older man slid a cue over. "You game?" Bob glanced at his watch. "Why not? Rules are simple—no more than five bucks a game, and I'm treating this like official duty." He rapped the table. "Deal?"

A ripple of chuckles, then nods all around. He chalked his cue and racked the balls. The table felt sturdy under his fingertips, the felt worn smooth. His first break was clean; two solids sank, leaving the stripes scattered. "Not bad for a cop," called one of the regulars. Bob shrugged, smiling. "I've had tougher cases."

The game proceeded with steady back-and-forth. Bob sank a tricky bank shot that drew a cheer. With each stroke, his mind unwound from protocol and paperwork—every shot a small celebration of precision and calm.

By the time the eight ball loomed, Bob was locked in concentration. He eyed the table: his solids were gone, only the eight remained. He lined up the shot, aimed for the corner pocket, and struck with measured grace. The eight dropped cleanly, and the table fell silent for a heartbeat before applause erupted. Bob stood, cue resting on his shoulder. "Good game, everyone," he said. He reached into his pocket and fished out a ten-dollar bill. "Ten bucks to spread around."

The group laughed and accepted the tip. Jake gave Bob a grateful nod. Bob patted Jake on the shoulder. "Keep practicing—and no more fights out here." Jake grinned. "You got it, officer." Bob walked back through the diner to collect his coffee, the buzz of friendly banter following him.

Tonight, at least, justice had a lighter side—and sometimes the best way to serve was to join the game. Bob wiped sweat from his brow under the neon glare as he returned to the table where Lou had set down his coffee. The aroma of fresh brew was a welcome contrast to the chalk dust lingering in the air. He inhaled deeply, savoring the moment of peace.

Just then, Marcy appeared again, balancing a tray of fries. "On the house," she said with a smile. "You look like you could use a refill." Bob nodded. "Thanks, Marcy." He took a fry and bit into the crisp saltiness. Behind him, the pool hall's door swung open as a trio of burly bikers swaggered in, leather jackets creaking. They carried an aura of trouble—one had a scar across his cheek, another a tattoo peeking from under his sleeve.

Bob's senses sharpened. He set down his fry and coined his coffee mug, standing slowly. "Looks like a busy night," he muttered. Sam frowned. "Those guys just roll in. Normally they mind their business." Bob followed their gaze. The bikers approached a corner table, laughter booming as they dropped helmets on chairs. One slammed a hand on the table. "We want a shot, cop," he barked, eyebrows cocked.

Bob stepped forward, hands visible. "I'm off duty. But I'll play fair or I'll clear the room. Your call." The scar-faced biker grinned, revealing a gold tooth. "Fine by me. Let's see what you've got." Bob retrieved his cue from the rack, chalking it methodically. He took his position. The first shot was tense—bikers jeered with each ball he sank. Bob's calm focus silenced them: a bank shot here, a combination there.

With a final soft click, Bob sank the eight ball behind his back, cue in one hand, the other tucked in pocket. The bikers stared, disbelief giving way to grudging respect. The scar-faced leader extended a hand. "Not bad, cop." Bob shook it. "Enjoy the game—but keep it clean."

As the bikers settled into an amicable post-game chat with Sam, Bob returned to his seat. Marcy placed a fresh coffee by his elbow. He smiled and raised his mug to her. "Thanks for watching my back." Marcy winked. "Anytime. Just another night at Joe's." Bob leaned back, fries in hand, and watched the lively scene. Off duty or not, part of him knew justice could wear many faces—even in the glow of a pool hall and the camaraderie of a shared game.

Bob finished his burger and fries, wiping his hands on a napkin before standing. The diner was quieter now, most patrons enthralled in the pool hall's action. He glanced at his watch—nearly midnight. He rose and stretched. "One more game?" he asked Sam, who shrugged with a grin. Bob grabbed his cue and returned to the table. Jake, Eric, and a few regulars had gathered for a friendly rematch. The felt was well-worn, the pockets stretched from countless games.

Bob racked the balls. "Let's make this last one count," he said with a wink. The shot was tight; Bob leaned in, eye level with the cue ball. He inhaled slowly and struck. The click of balls hitting was soft but confident—one striped ball sank exactly where he intended. Jake clapped. "You're on fire tonight, officer!"

Bob just smiled and continued, each shot a steady rhythm. Conversation flowed easily—tips on bank shots, laughter at a miscue. For these moments, Bob was just one of the gang, not the law enforcing peace. The eight ball rolled toward the corner pocket. Bob tracked its path and called his shot. With perfect finesse, he sank it. "Game!" he announced, standing. The group cheered.

Bob gathered his winnings—a few crumpled dollar bills—and folded them into his pocket. "Good playing, everyone. Keep practicing." As he turned to leave, Jake stopped him. "Thanks for tonight, Officer Bob. You reminded us that sometimes it's about more than winning." Bob nodded, touched. "Remember that." He tipped an imaginary hat and headed back toward the diner's counter. Marcy smiled as he passed. "Closing time soon, officer."

Bob waved. "One last coffee, please. And thanks—for keeping this place homey." She refilled his cup. Bob sipped, content. The lights dimmed slightly, signaling the end of another night. He glanced back at the pool hall, its neon glow fading into the diner's warmth. For Bob, justice meant more than arrests—it meant community, respect, and the simple joy of a game well played.

Bob lingered by the pool table, the aftermath of the game still warm in the air. He gathered cue and chalk, slipping them into their rack slot. The others began to drift away—some clutching pool cues, others their winnings and beers. Sam approached, wiping his hands on a towel. "Have you ever thought of going pro?" he teased. Bob chuckled. "I'll stick to keeping the peace." He patted Sam on the shoulder. "Thanks for the game—and the break."

Outside, the midnight breeze was cool and damp. Bob stepped back into his cruiser, the engine purring as he settled behind the wheel. He reached for his radio. "Bob to dispatch—night watch complete. No further incidents." A crackle and a sleepy "Copy that" came through. He drove home along empty streets, neon signs fading into the rearview mirror.

His mind replayed the evening: teens learning respect, bikers sharing quiet camaraderie, and a simple game bringing everyone together. Pulling into his driveway, Bob cut the engine and sat for a moment, the hum of the city muted. He unbuckled his seatbelt and reached into the passenger seat for his notebook. Flicking to a blank page, he wrote:

> *"Sometimes the smallest shifts—an eight-ball banked, a teen given guidance—make the biggest difference. Justice wears many faces."*

He snapped the notebook shut, turned off the dome light, and stepped into the house. The door clicked softly behind him. Bob's slippers squeaked on the kitchen tile as he poured a glass of water. He paused at the fridge, the night's thoughts still swirling—justice, community, connection. He carried his coffee from earlier to the living room, where a stack of case files waited. But tonight, he let them lie. Settling into his favorite armchair, Bob flipped open his notebook to the page with the pool hall reflection. He re-read the words, a faint smile playing on his lips:

> *"Justice wears many faces."*

He closed the book and leaned back, the soft hum of the refrigerator the only sound. Tomorrow, the files will be called. But tonight, he savored the glow of camaraderie and the simple truth that sometimes, peace came in the form of a well-played game.

Later that night, a soft knock at the door jolted Bob from sleep. He glanced at the clock—2:17 AM. Who could be calling at this hour? Stepping quietly, he opened the door a crack. There stood Marcy, her expression anxious, uniform damp from rain. "Officer Bob—I'm sorry to wake you," she whispered. "It's about the bikers… one of them got tossed from his bike near the bridge. He's hurt, and I thought you should know."

Bob's training snapped on. He grabbed his coat. "Lead the way." Marcy guided him to her patrol car down the street. Lights painted the wet pavement red and blue. At the bridge's railing, the scar-faced biker lay on a stretcher, paramedics working to stabilize him. Bob knelt beside him. "What happened?" A paramedic replied, "He lost control around the bend—overcorrected, went off the road. He's alive but needs surgery." Bob sighed, relieved it wasn't worse. He looked at Marcy. "Good thing you called." Marcy nodded. "I couldn't just let it go."

Bob helped direct traffic until the ambulance pulled away. Then, as the rain eased, he and Marcy stood under the bridge's arch. "You saved a life tonight," Marcy said softly. Bob's gaze lifted to the dark sky. "Guess justice found me again." By dawn's first light, Bob was back home, the adrenaline of the night spent. He showered quickly, then brewed a strong pot of coffee, each sip grounding him.

He scribbled a brief note in his journal:

> *"Tonight reminded me that duty never rests—even when you think it does. Every call matters."*

He placed the notebook on his bedside table and climbed back into bed, the sheets cool against his skin. Sleep came swiftly, the weight of the world eased by kindness, a game well played, and the silent promise to stand watch. Morning sunlight filtered through the curtains as Bob woke to his alarm. He dressed in his uniform, pinning on the badge that had guided him through standoffs, chases, and even pool-hall showdowns. Downstairs, his spouse had left a note on the kitchen table:

> *"Coffee's on. Tell me everything when you get home. Love, Sarah."*

Bob smiled, heart warmed. He filled a travel mug and kissed the note. "All right," he said aloud, "time to get back to work." He stepped out, locked the door, and headed toward his cruiser—mind already scanning the day's calls. Whether in the heat of action or the calm before dawn, Officer Bob was ready for whatever story came next.

Chapter 5: The Great Llama Escape

It was an ordinary Sunday afternoon when dispatch crackled in Bob's cruiser: "We've got reports of a loose llama on Main Street, eastbound." Bob almost laughed—until he saw the chaos through his windshield. Horns blared as cars swerved around something large and woolly bounding down the road. He flicked on his lights and pulled up alongside a bewildered family in a minivan. "What happened?" Bob called over the siren's drone.

The driver—wide-eyed—pointed. "It just appeared out of nowhere! Knocked down our trash cans, ran through the grocery store parking lot, now it's heading for the park!" Bob leaped from the car, radio clipped to his vest. Nearby pedestrians scattered as the llama bounded past, its thick fleece shimmering in the afternoon sun. Bob jogged after it, adrenaline kicking in. "Unit 14 to dispatch—we're on foot pursuit of a llama, moving toward Lincoln Park," he reported, chasing down the runaway "suspect." The llama turned a corner, half-spooking a jogger, then darted between parked cars. Bob gauged the distance—about twenty yards—then called softly, "Easy now… steady…"

He slipped his radio aside and drew a coil of rope from his cruiser—something he'd learned from animal-control training. With practiced ease, Bob approached the llama's line of sight, voice calm: "Hey there, buddy... I've got some help for you." The llama skidded to a halt, ears pricked. Bob slowed, arm outstretched, the rope loop coiled in his hand like a lasso. He spoke in a low tone, inching closer: "It's okay. Let's get you back home."

The animal seemed to sense Bob's calm, inching toward him. Bob knelt, gently placing the loop over the llama's neck. With one smooth tug, he secured the lead. A small cheer rose from bystanders as Bob guided the llama away from traffic, heading for the awaiting animal-control truck. The animal-control officer, Reyes, hurried over, sliding open the truck's back gate. "Nice work, Bob," she said, clipping the rope securely to the llama's halter. The llama nudged Bob's hand, soft fleece brushing his glove.

Bob smiled. "Name's Lenny, right?" he asked, reading the small tag hanging from the halter. Reyes nodded. "Lenny's been spooked—escaped from a local petting zoo after a loose gate. The kid's birthday party went wrong." Bob climbed the truck's steps and helped guide Lenny inside. "Let's get you back before someone else mistakes you for a woolly road hazard."

Reyes secured the llama and hopped down. "You want to ride shotgun back to the zoo?" she offered with a grin. Bob waved off the offer. "I've got paperwork to file—plus, I promised Mrs. Caldwell I'd drop by." "Mrs. Caldwell?" Reyes asked as Bob headed back to his cruiser. "Neighbor," Bob explained, checking his radio. "Her grandson's birthday party devolved into an all-out llama sprint. She's worried sick."

He climbed into his cruiser, the engine's rumble comforting after the chase. "Unit 14 to dispatch, llama secured, returning to Mrs. Caldwell's." He navigated the streets, a smile tugging at his lips. As the zoo's plaque came into view—"Green Valley Petting Zoo"—Bob slowed. He watched Reyes lead Lenny into a fenced enclosure where children waved excitedly. Lenny ambled toward his pen, ears flicking contentedly. Bob stepped out, striding over to the enclosure gate. Mrs. Caldwell, a petite woman with silver-streaked hair, rushed forward. "Thank you, Officer Bob," she exclaimed. "You have no idea what a relief this is."

Bob tipped his hat. "Just doing my job, ma'am. Happy birthday to your grandson." She smiled and waved as Bob walked back to his cruiser, the afternoon sun warming his back. He settled into the driver's seat, the image of children's laughter echoing in his mind.

Bob settled in at his desk that afternoon, the image of Lenny safely back at the petting zoo lingering in his thoughts. He opened his incident log and began typing:

> **Incident Report #2025-0512**
> **Animal:** Lenny the Llama
> **Location:** Main Street → Lincoln Park → Green Valley Petting Zoo
> **Outcome:** Llama safely returned; no injuries reported.

He paused to sip his coffee, then added:

> **Notes:**
>
> - Initial sighting near grocery lot.
>
> - Successful rope capture with minimal stress to animals.
>
> - Petting zoo gate malfunction confirmed; recommended follow-up with city animal control.

Bob closed the report and printed a copy for Reyes. He walked over to the K-9 office, where Reyes was filing her own paperwork. "Here you go," he said, handing her the printout. "We should recommend they inspect that gate—Lenny's lucky nobody got hurt." Reyes glanced at the form and nodded. "Will do. You really have a way with animals, Bob."

He smiled. "A little training goes a long way." He patted Scout, who had wandered in for a visit. The German Shepherd wagged his tail, ready for the next adventure. Later, Bob checked his watch—still hours before his shift ended. He stepped outside into the late afternoon sun, inhaling the scent of rain-washed pavement. His next call awaited, but for now, he allowed himself a moment's pride: today, a runaway llama became the highlight of the week.

That evening, as twilight painted the sky in purples and golds, Bob guided Lenny's harnessed trailer through quiet neighborhood streets. He had volunteered to help Reyes return the trailer after hours so she could finish paperwork uninterrupted. Lenny munched calmly on hay, nostrils flaring with each gentle breath. Bob hummed a soft tune, glancing at the llama in the mirror. "You were quite the escape artist today, weren't you?" Lenny blinked, as if in agreement.

They arrived at the city animal-control yard, where fading daylight cast long shadows across rows of empty pens. Reyes stood waiting, holding a lantern. "Thanks for the lift," she said. "I owe you one." Bob unhitched the trailer and opened the gate. Lenny stepped out gracefully, sniffing the cold ground. Bob led him to his pen, where hay and fresh water awaited. Reyes flicked on the lantern's beam and smiled. "Looks like he's home."

Bob patted Lenny's neck. "Sleep well, buddy." He dusted hay from his hands and turned to Reyes. "Drive safe," she called as he climbed into his cruiser. Bob rolled the windows down and breathed in the crisp night air. Lenny's adventure was over, but the memory of wide eyes and bounding legs stayed with him—another story for the books.

The next morning, Bob arrived at the station early, still thinking about Lenny's wide-eyed run through Main Street. He poured himself a cup of coffee and flipped open his notebook:

> **Reflection:**
> *Sometimes the oddest calls—like chasing a llama—remind me why I love this job. It's never dull.*

He tucked the notebook into his jacket pocket just as Reyes walked in, rubbing her eyes with a grin. "Did you get up early or just never left?" she teased."Couldn't sleep," Bob admitted. "That llama chase got me buzzing." Reyes nodded. "Good work yesterday. I filed the gate-repair request before I left. The petting zoo manager called—"you may get a thank-you note." Bob laughed. "I'll frame it." He grabbed his radio. "Unit 14 to all units—remember to report any more exotic escapes. Officer Bob's llama hotline remains open."

A chuckle spread through the room as Bob and Reyes headed to roll call. Outside, Scout trotted by, ready for the day's patrol. Bob clipped on Scout's leash and patted his head. "Let's see what's next, partner." Bob and Scout began their patrol under a crisp morning sky, the city stirring to life. As they approached Maple Avenue, an urgent call came over the radio: "Unit 14, we have a report of a child's birthday party at Elm Park—possible runaway llama sighting. Be advised."

Bob exchanged a grin with Scout and replied, "On my way." They jogged toward Elm Park, where clusters of balloons marked the party area. Families gathered, faces animated. In the center of the lawn, children giggled as a young llama—possibly Lenny's cousin—bounded among the tables, nibbling on streamers. A frantic parent chased after, arms flailing. Bob knelt in the grass and spoke softly, "Hey there, friend. Let's get you back." The llama paused, ears swiveling. Scout approached calmly, gently guiding the animal toward Bob. With one practiced loop of rope, Bob secured the llama's halter. The parent exhaled in relief. "Thank you! I don't know how it got loose!"

Bob offered a warm smile. "They find the smallest gaps. I'll stay until Animal Control arrives." Families clapped as Bob led the llama back to the fenced area by the park gate. When the animal-control truck pulled up, Bob stepped aside and patted Scout. "Great teamwork, buddy." The children waved enthusiastically as the llama climbed safely into the back of the truck.

Bob watched the truck depart, a light breeze carrying the sound of birthday laughter. Another unusual call, another story added to the book of Officer Bob's adventures. Later that afternoon, Bob returned to the precinct and found his partner John tapping away at a keyboard. "How's it going?" Bob asked, setting his notebook on the desk. John looked up. "All reports filed—Lenny's gate is fixed, and Elm Park cleaned up. You're trending in department chat: 'Llama Whisperer.'" He chuckled.

Bob rolled his eyes with a grin. "Happy to hold the title. What's next on the docket?" John pointed to the monitor. "We've a noise complaint at the docks—possible crate smash. Could be our warehouse crew from last week." Bob sighed. "Alright, let's sort that out." He grabbed his coat and patted Scout, who sprang up eagerly.

As they headed out, Bob reflected on how a simple Sunday chase had turned into a series of memorable rescues. He climbed into the cruiser and started the engine, ready to add the next chapter—create noise or not—to his ever-growing book of untold adventures. Back in his office late that evening, Bob flicked on the desk lamp and stacked the day's reports—Main Street chase, zoo return, Elm Park rescue, follow-up memo. He opened his notebook to a blank page:

> **Chapter Reflection:**
> *Today showed me that "policing" isn't always about crime and punishment. Sometimes it's about keeping the neighborhood safe in unexpected ways—like rescuing a llama in full sprint.*

He tapped his pen against the page, thinking of Lenny's gentle eyes and the children's laughter at the birthday party. Scout nosed his elbow, reminding him it was time to wrap up. Bob closed the notebook and leaned back, letting the quiet of the station settle around him. Tomorrow would bring new calls, new challenges—but tonight, he carried the warmth of a community coming together over an unlikely crisis.

He switched off the lamp, leaving the reflection to linger in the soft glow of the monitor. As he walked out, he whispered to the empty room, "Another story told." The next morning, Bob arrived at the precinct early, greeted by the quiet hum of computers and the scent of fresh coffee. He hung his coat, patted Scout's head, and poured a cup before settling at his desk. Across the station PA, dispatch called units to their assignments, but Bob took a moment. He opened his notebook to the llama chapter and added one final note:

> *"Memorable moments often come unannounced. Today, I'm grateful for every odd call that reminds me how varied—and wonderful—this job can be."*

He closed the book and stood, stretching as the station began to buzz. Scanning the schedule, he spotted a community outreach meeting later that afternoon—a chance to share Lenny's tale with local schools and animal groups. Bob smiled. "Let's teach them to be ready for the unexpected," he murmured to Scout, who wagged in agreement. He gathered his things, heading out to turn one more unsung story into a lesson for the neighborhood.

That evening, Bob addressed a small group of elementary students and parents at the local community center. A slideshow flickered behind him: images of Lenny bounding down Main Street, Scout guiding the llama, and children cheering at Elm Park. "Sometimes," Bob told the crowd, "heroes aren't just about arrests or big emergencies. They're about compassion, creativity, and keeping each other safe—whether the problem is a runaway llama or something far more serious."

Hands shot up with questions: "How did you catch him?" "Weren't you scared?" Bob answered each with warmth and humor, encouraging respect for animals and for the men and women who serve. Afterward, children lined up to pet Scout and pose for photos with a plush llama mascot he'd borrowed from the petting zoo. Bob watched their laughter echo in the hall, feeling a deep sense of purpose.

Driving home that night, with Scout curled in the passenger seat, Bob reflected on Chapter 5—how a simple unexpected call became a lesson in community and care. He flipped open his notebook one last time and added:

> *"Today's lesson: embrace every story. You never know whose life you might brighten."*

He snapped the notebook shut, the glow of the dashboard lights reflecting in his eyes. Tomorrow would bring the next untold adventure—and he was ready.

Chapter 6: Midnight Rescue at Cedar Rapids

The radio crackled at 2:03 AM:

> "Units 14 and 18—possible water rescue needed on Cedar Creek Road. Floodwaters are rising fast. Exercise extreme caution."

Bob swung his legs over the edge of his bed, heart already pounding. He threw on his turnout gear—waterproof jacket, boots, life vest—grabbed his helmet and radio, and sprinted to the cruiser. The drive was a blur of dark country roads and warning lights. Rain sluiced down the windshield, turning the world into streaks of red and blue. Bob's wipers fought for traction, but the deluge was relentless.

He arrived at Cedar Creek Road to find a scene of controlled chaos: headlights bobbing, officers directing traffic, and the distant roar of churning water. Orange flood barriers lay half-submerged, warning tape fluttered in the wind. Bob checked his watch—2:12 AM—and clipped his radio back on. "Bob to Command: I'm on scene. What's the status?" A voice replied: "Family trapped in camper at mile marker 7. Water reached the axles. Two adults, two kids. SWAT boat on the way." Bob pressed his lips into a thin line.

He grabbed his helmet and waded through knee-deep water toward the camper's rooftop, where silhouettes clung to the railing. "Stay calm!" he called. "We're coming for you!" The family's voices rose in hopeful shouts. Bob scanned the swirling current—debris, hidden eddies, and the ominous pull of the creek's center.

He took a breath, remembering every water-rescue drill he'd ever run. He tethered a rope to his belt, secured it at the bank, and signaled to the awaiting boat crew. "Deploy!" he yelled as the inflatable boat sliced through the black water toward the camper's side. Bob braced himself on the slick bank, ready to guide the boat into the tempest...

The inflatable rescue boat rocked violently as it approached the camper. Bob waded deeper, gripping the side rail with one hand while steadying himself against the current. Water splashed over the bow, cold and unforgiving. Inside the camper's doorway stood a man holding a flashlight in one hand and his terrified daughter in the other. Beside him, his wife clung to their young son. Bob locked eyes with the father. "Sir, grab my hand and guide your daughter into the boat," Bob instructed, voice firm over the wind's howl. The man complied, carefully lowering the child over the boat's rail.

Bob helped her into a seat, then turned to the mother. "Step down here, and I'll lift your son in." He scooped up the boy, cradling him against his vest as the woman climbed aboard beside her. With both children safe, Bob reached for the father. The man hesitated, panic in his eyes. Bob offered a steadying hand and a nod. "I've got you." Together, they climbed in, the boat's bow dipping under the extra weight.

A crewman grunted, rowing hard against the current, while Bob held the family close. Every jostle of the boat felt magnified in the churning water. The camper's roof slipped from view as they edged downstream toward safety. Finally, the bank loomed near, a swirl of muddy water rushing past their legs. Bob helped unload the family, each member's relief palpable as they collapsed on drier ground. He checked them over—no injuries beyond shock and cold. "Thank you," the mother whispered, voice thick with gratitude. Bob nodded, wet hair plastered to his forehead. "Let's get you warm and checked by medics." He motioned to the waiting paramedics. As blankets were wrapped around the family and they were led to an awaiting ambulance, Bob stood at the water's edge, adrenaline still coursing. The rescue was complete—but the night was far from over.

Bob peeled off his waterlogged gloves and surveyed the scene. Floodlights illuminated the swollen creek, its surface rippling with debris—from branches to stray garbage bins—each obstacle a hidden threat. The rescue boat crew secured their vessel on the bank, nodding at Bob in silent acknowledgment of a job well done.

He checked his watch—2:30 AM—and then spotted the camper's stranded vehicle, its windows darkened by the storm. The driver's side door hung open as if in a silent plea for closure. Bob knew his work wasn't finished until the scene was secured and no one remained at risk. He returned the family's leads to dispatch: "Unit 14: family accounted for and transferred to medics. Proceeding to secure the camper." A crackle responded: "Copy that. Backup en route."

Bob made his way back into the knee-high water, careful with each step. The creek's undercurrent tugged at him, but his boots held firm. Reaching the camper, he secured the door, ensuring it wouldn't swing open with the surging water. He tied a tether rope from the vehicle to a nearby tree, preventing further drift. As he worked, Bob felt a tingle of satisfaction welling in his chest. Tonight's mission had been a test of skill, courage, and resolve—and he'd passed.

The roar of the creek began to fade under the hum of arriving units, radios crackling with updates and instructions. Bob climbed back onto dry land, brushing mud from his jacket. He looked toward the ambulance lights flickering in the distance. Another chapter closed, another family safe. He wrapped his arms around himself against the chill. He glanced at Scout, who trotted up with a wagging tail, ready for whatever came next. Bob patted his partner's head and whispered, "Good work, buddy. Let's call it a night."

By 3:00 AM, the last of the medical teams had departed, and Bob and Scout trudged back to the cruiser, boots squelching against soaked gravel. He shook raindrops from his jacket and leaned inside to grab a towel from the backseat. He tucked the towel around Scout's neck to dry the dog's fur, then patted it off on his own sleeve. "Let's head back," he murmured, surveying the flooded roadway now cordoned off with warning lights and reflective cones. Back at the station, he logged the final details: "Secured camper, tied to tree for stability. All civilians safe and transferred to medical care." He sent the update and closed his laptop, exhaustion tugging at his eyelids. Scout nosed his hand, reminding him it was time for their walk.

Bob clipped on the leash and stepped outside into a clearing sky, where the wind had stilled and stars peeked through thinning clouds. They walked down the quiet street leading to his home. Each step felt heavy, the weight of the night's rescue still echoing in his bones. Yet with every breath of cool night air, Bob felt a steady calm returning.

Halfway home, he paused by a lamppost, letting Scout sniff at the grass. Bob looked up at the moonlit sky and whispered, "Another story told." Then, with Scout by his side, he finished the short trek to his front porch and headed inside to rest. Bob slipped off his soaked boots in the locker room and collapsed onto a bench. He peeled off his wet jacket, draping it over a hook, and pulled his leather notebook from his pocket. Flicking to a fresh page, he began to write:

June 13, 2:45 AM
Cedar Creek Road Rescue

- Family of four rescued from flooded camper

- Water depth reached vehicle axles; strong undercurrent

- No injuries beyond shock and hypothermia

- **Reflection:**
 Tonight reminded me why we train for worst-case scenarios. When seconds count, calm efficiency matters more than adrenaline. Scout was a rock—never hesitated once.

Lessons Learned:

1. Always tether civilian vehicles during floods.

2. Use quiet commands when chaos reigns.

3. After action, always check the family for delayed shock symptoms.

Closing Thought:
 In darkness and storm, hope finds a way.

He tapped the pen, rereading his words. Outside, the first light of dawn stained the station windows pale pink. Bob snapped the notebook shut, slipping it back into his coat. Changing into dry uniform pants, he knew paperwork and debrief awaited—but for now, he carried the silent pride of another life safeguarded. By first light, Bob joined the morning roll call in the briefing room, uniform crisp and notebook in hand. Lieutenant Ramirez tapped his badge against the table. "Heard about the creek rescue last night—good work, Bob." Bob nodded and distributed copies of his incident report to the team. "Family rescued without injury, camper secured. Key takeaway: tether every stranded vehicle and move quickly when waters rise."

Questions followed—officers asking about currents, rope angles, and Scout's deployment. Bob answered each, demonstrating his knot technique and sharing the calm commands he used under pressure. After the debrief, Bob headed to his desk to file final paperwork. He updated the department's rescue protocols with lessons learned and attached a link to his notebook entry for reference. Dispatch notified him of another call—a late-night noise complaint downtown—but Bob paused. Today, he reflected, was about mastering preparation as much as responding.

He sipped a fresh cup of coffee and watched Scout trot by, ready for the next assignment. Bob closed his laptop and penned one last note in his notebook:

> *"In every rescue, the smallest detail—where to tie a rope, how to read the water—can mean the difference between harm and hope. Stay prepared, stay calm."*

With that, he clipped the notebook and radio to his belt, ready to carry the next untold story forward. Late that afternoon, Bob found himself back at Cedar Creek Road, this time under bright sunlight and calm skies. A follow-up team had arrived to inspect the flooded zone and remove the warning barriers. Bob stood beside the creek, Scout at his side, watching technicians test the current with measuring sticks. A familiar voice called out—Mrs. Thompson, the camper's mother, approached with her daughter toddling beside her. The girl ran into Bob's arms, squealing, "Thank you, Officer Bob!" The mother's eyes brimmed as she shook his hand. Bob knelt to the girl's level and smiled. "Stay safe, okay? And remember, always wait for help." He patted her head gently. Turning to Mrs. Thompson, he handed her his business card. "If you need anything—medical follow-up or just to talk—don't hesitate."

She nodded gratefully. "You saved our family tonight—can't thank you enough." Bob stood, scanning the creek's now-tranquil surface. "Just doing my job. I'm glad you're all right." Mrs. Thompson waved goodbye, and they walked away hand in hand. Bob turned back to the water, patting Scout's head. Together, they watched as the follow-up crew raised the barriers and began pumping out the remaining water, knowing their midnight work would help prevent future emergencies.

With a final glance at the creek's steady flow, Bob pocketed his notebook and headed toward his cruiser—another chapter of duty complete, and another life protected. Bob slipped out of his soaked gear in the locker room and draped it over the drying rack. He carried his notebook and pen back to the briefing room, where Lieutenant Ramirez waited with a steaming mug of coffee. "I figured you might need this," Ramirez said, handing it over. Bob accepted with a grateful nod. Bob opened his notebook to the Cedar Creek entry and added one final reflection:

> *"In the darkness and roar of floodwaters, every second counts. Tonight, trust in training—and in Scout—made all the difference."*

He closed the notebook and stood, stretching muscles stiff from the cold water. Ramirez placed a hand on his shoulder. "Your report has already influenced our flood-response protocol. We'll be adding tether points along Cedar Creek Road." Bob smiled, warmed by the news. "Glad to help. Let me know if you need anything else." Ramirez nodded. "Get some rest, Bob. We'll handle the aftermath."

As Bob walked out into the dawning light, Scout at his heels, he felt the familiar pull of duty and the quiet pride of a rescue well done. Ahead lay new calls, new stories—but for now, he carried the satisfaction of knowing a family's worst night had a safe ending. By evening, Bob found a quiet moment in the station's break room. The adrenaline of the rescue had faded into a gentle hum of satisfaction, replaced now by hunger and a stiff back. He poured himself a cup of coffee and opened his notebook to the Cedar Creek entry.

> **After Action Reflection:**
> *Today proved that even in darkness and chaos, preparation shines brightest. Every knot tied, every command given, and every step taken with care turned panic into safety.*

He jotted down a few reminders for future training drills—ropes practice, K-9 coordination, rapid medical checks—and closed the notebook with a soft snap. The station's overhead lights hummed as he stretched, readying himself for the final duties of the day. A cheerful bark beside him signaled Scout's approval. Bob clipped the leash back on, rose, and headed for the door. Outside, the night air was cool and calm—a stark contrast to the tempest of hours before. With Scout at his side, Bob walked back toward the locker room, whispering one last line: "Another story told."

The station was quiet as Bob returned from roll call, Scout padding beside him on leash. He paused outside his office, notebook in hand, and reflected on the night's work—how a family's plight had led him into roaring waters and back again. He opened the final blank page reserved for Cedar Creek and wrote:

> **Closing Reflection:**
> *Flooded roads can break more than vehicles—they can break spirits. In those darkest moments, a steady hand and clear mind can rebuild hope.*

Bob snapped the notebook shut and tucked it into his coat. He glanced at Scout, whose tail wagged with quiet pride. Together, they walked through the station's corridors—past trophy cases of old commendations and walls lined with dispatch monitors—each a reminder of the many stories held within these walls. Outside, the moon cast a pale glow over the cruiser parked below. Bob loaded Scout into the passenger seat and climbed in, securing his seatbelt. As the engine hummed to life, he thought of the countless pages still waiting to be written—chapters of courage, compassion, and community.

Chapter 7: Training Rookie Chad

Driving into the night, headlights cutting a path through the darkness, Bob whispered to the empty road, "Another story told." Bob arrived at roll call to find Rookie Chad standing nervously by the briefing table. The young officer's uniform hung loosely, and his eyes flickered around the room like a deer caught in headlights. Bob gave him a reassuring nod. "Morning, Chad," he said warmly. "Ready for your first full shift with me?" Chad straightened, swallowing hard. "Yes, sir. I'm ready to learn." Bob clapped him on the shoulder. "Good. Today we're focusing on traffic stops—approach technique, radio procedure, and de-escalation. I'll talk you through each step. Stay close, listen up, and don't be afraid to ask questions." As Lieutenant Ramirez wrapped up the briefing, Bob hooked his radio to his belt and turned to Chad. "Ever been to a high-speed pursuit?" Chad's eyes widened. "No, sir. I've only observed simulators." Bob smiled. "Then today's a good day to take notes—lucky for us, I don't plan on any real chases. Let's roll." Bob steered the cruiser onto Pine Avenue, spotting a beat-up sedan weaving between lanes below the speed limit. He tapped his mic: "Dispatch, this is Unit 14. Request a routine traffic stop on vehicle 5-Delta—plate reads XJ3-89T."

Chad's voice crackled back, excitement tempered by nerves: "Copy that, Unit 14." Bob flipped on the overhead lights and eased behind the sedan. The driver glanced in the mirror, eyebrows raised, then signaled a turn onto a side street. Bob guided them to a gentle stop, cutting the engine before exiting the vehicle. "Approach on the passenger side," Bob instructed, nodding to Chad. They advanced in unison—Bob slightly ahead, Chad close behind at a 45° angle. Bob tapped the window. The driver—an elderly man—lowered the glass. "Officer, what seems to be the problem?" Bob offered a calm smile. "Good evening, sir. I'm Officer Bob, and this is Officer Chad. We pulled you over for erratic lane changes. May I see your license and registration, please?"

Chad watched intently as Bob gently extended his hand for the documents. The driver fumbled in his glovebox, producing a worn wallet and handing over a license. Bob thanked him and stepped back to confer quietly with Chad. "Notice his hands were slow but steady—good sign. We'll check for impairment but likely a mechanical issue." Chad nodded, pen poised over his ticket book. Bob returned the license. "Everything checks out, sir. Your turn signal is out—didn't mean to panic you, right?" The man chuckled ruefully. "No, officer. I didn't even realize."

Bob handed him a warning citation and offered a card. "Here's a repair shop we recommend. Get that signal fixed, and you'll be back to safe driving in no time. You're free to go." As the driver eased back onto the road, Chad exhaled. Bob patted his shoulder. "Solid work—staying calm, watching his hands, clear communication. That's how you build trust." Chad's grin stretched ear to ear. "Thanks, sir. It feels good to help without drama." Bob nodded. "Traffic stops are everyday opportunities to keep people safe—and to teach the next generation how it's done." Bob guided the cruiser toward the industrial park, where dispatch had flagged a possible break-in alarm at Suncrest Warehousing. "Chad, keep an eye on the surveillance monitors while I check the perimeter," he instructed as they arrived.

Chad nodded and tapped the in-car console, pulling up grainy CCTV feeds. Shadows moved between loading docks, vans idling. "Looks like someone's near Dock 3," Chad reported, voice low with anticipation. Bob slipped on his tactical gloves and stepped into the cool night air, flashlight in hand. The beam cut through the darkness, revealing rows of stacked pallets and metal doors. He moved silently, boots crunching on gravel. Chad stayed inside, narrating, "I see you near the east corner—two figures, crouched." Bob crept closer, staying in cover. He spotted the intruders—young men prying at a container lock. He tapped his mic: "Chad, suspect activity confirmed. Two suspects tampering with a container at Dock 3. I'm moving in." Chad's voice was steady: "Copy that. Backup en route—ETA two minutes." Bob edged to within ten feet, flashlight trained on the lock. He called out: "Police! Hands where I can see them!" The figures froze. One fumbled a crowbar; the other raised his hands. Bob stepped forward, voice firm but calm: "Drop the tools and get on your knees." They complied, the crowbar clattering on the concrete. Bob cuffed the first suspect while keeping his light on the second. "Why break in here?" he asked.

The suspects muttered about a quick score—illicit electronics hidden in crates. Bob radioed: "Unit 14 to dispatch—two in custody, stolen goods recovered. Send transport." Chad opened the door. "Need a hand, sir?" Bob nodded. "Bring the evidence bags." Together they processed the scene, tagging recovered items and reading Miranda rights to the suspects. Back in the cruiser, Chad exhaled. "That was intense." Bob offered a tight smile. "Good instincts. Remember—clear commands, control the light, and back yourself up with tech." He patted Chad's shoulder. "You're doing great."

Bob and Chad arrived back at the precinct just before dawn. Chad carried the evidence bags into the booking area while Bob completed the booking report on his handheld terminal. Each item—the crowbar, the lock pick set, the recovered electronics—was catalogued and tagged.

Once the paperwork was done, Bob led Chad upstairs to the armory. "Let's review your first use of force and de-escalation," Bob said, gesturing to a training dummy. He walked Chad through the proper stance, control holds, and verbal commands used during the warehouse arrest. Chad practiced each move under Bob's watchful eye. When Chad hesitated on the final control hold, Bob stepped in, adjusting his grip and demonstrating the fluid motion. Chad repeated it until it felt natural. "Remember," Bob said, "it's not about overpowering—it's about managing the situation safely. You did great tonight, but always refine your technique."

Chad nodded, wiping sweat from his brow. "Thank you, sir. I feel more confident already." Bob clapped him on the back. "That's why we train. Now let's grab some coffee before the roll call—today's going to be a long one." Later that morning, Bob and Chad joined the department's weekly training seminar in the conference room.

A slideshow displayed best practices for traffic stops, courtroom testimony, and use-of-force reports. Chad settled into a chair beside Bob, notebook open. Detective Morales clicked to the next slide: **"Building Rapport & Community Trust."** Chad shot Bob a glance, as if to say, "We've got this." Bob whispered, "Stick to what you know—listen first, then act."

As Morales spoke, Bob nudged Chad toward asking a question about de-escalation tactics. Chad cleared his throat and inquired, "How do you balance authority with empathy during a tense stop?" Morales paused, then praised the question: "Great point. You start by stating your role clearly, then acknowledge the person's perspective—'I understand you may be in a hurry…' That small step diffuses tension."

Chad made a note as Bob gave him an approving nod. After the seminar, Bob led Chad outside to a mock "community engagement" exercise—greeting volunteers posing as residents with concerns about local traffic. "Remember your opening line," Bob reminded him. "Introduce yourself, state the purpose, then listen." Chad approached a middle-aged woman standing by a makeshift neighborhood sign. He extended his hand. "Good afternoon, ma'am.

I'm Officer Chad with the local precinct. I understand you've expressed concerns about speeding on Elm Street—may I hear more?" The volunteer relaxed and began detailing her worries. Bob watched proudly as Chad listened intently, asked follow-up questions, and offered realistic solutions. When the exercise concluded, the volunteer commended Chad on his professionalism. Bob patted Chad's shoulder. "See? Empathy and clear communication go a long way." Chad grinned. "Thanks, Officer Bob. I'm learning from the best."

Back in the cruiser, Bob powered up the mobile terminal and opened the incident report Chad had begun drafting. "Writing good reports is as important as making arrests," Bob reminded him. He scrolled through Chad's narrative of the warehouse break-in:

> *"At approximately 2345 hours, I observed two suspects prying at Dock 3..."*

Bob tapped a line. "Good start, but let's add sensory details—what did you hear when they froze? How did the wind shift as you drew your light? These details help the jury picture the scene."

Chad nodded and retyped:

> *"The crunch of gravel underfoot alerted me before I saw the suspects. A cold wind rushed past as I called out, 'Police! Hands where I can see them!'"*

"Perfect," Bob said. "Now check your evidence chain." He walked Chad through tagging the crowbar: serial number, location found, who handled it. "If any link breaks, that item can be ruled inadmissible." Chad's brow furrowed thoughtfully. "So every transfer—from scene to evidence bag to station—needs documentation?" Bob smiled. "Exactly. Treat each step like a relay race baton. One slip and the handoff fails." Chad updated the chain-of-custody log. Bob reviewed and signed off. He patted Chad on the back. "You're building solid habits. Keep this up, and you'll be writing textbook-worthy reports." As they glanced ahead at the next shift assignment—neighborhood patrol—Bob said, "Ready for your first solo neighborhood check?" Chad straightened in his seat. "Absolutely, sir." Bob nodded. "I'll ride with you, but I'll let you take the lead. I'll be right behind, ready if you need me." Chad exhaled, excitement and nerves in equal measure. Bob started the engine. "Let's go make a positive difference." Chad sat up straighter as Bob parked on Willow Lane, the first stop on their neighborhood patrol. "All right, Chad—your turn," Bob said, sliding his sunglasses off the dashboard. "Introduce yourself and ask if there are any concerns." Chad opened his door and stepped onto the sidewalk, approaching a woman tending her front garden. He cleared his throat. "Good afternoon, ma'am. Officer Chad, here with Officer Bob.

We're checking in to see if you've noticed any suspicious activity or safety issues on Willow Lane lately." The woman looked up, pleasantly surprised. "Oh, hello, Officer Chad. Well, actually, we've had a few cars speeding down here in the mornings." She gestured toward the street. "It's dangerous when the kids wait for the school bus." Chad nodded. "Thank you. That's helpful. I'll note the times and dates of the incidents and discuss possible speed bumps or increased signage with dispatch." He made initial notes in his pad. "Anything else you'd like to mention?" She smiled. "No, that's it for now. Thank you for checking in." Chad returned to the cruiser. Bob gave him an approving glance. "Nicely done—courteous, thorough, and you addressed her concerns with real solutions."

They continued down the block, Chad taking the lead on two more stops: a report of stray dogs in a yard (he coordinated Animal Control) and a broken streetlight (he logged it for maintenance). At each home, he maintained eye contact, listened carefully, and offered clear next steps. On the final call, Chad radioed in his findings. Bob leaned over and whispered, "You handled all that solo—great initiative." Chad exhaled, a proud grin spreading.

Bob started the engine. "Ready for your debrief?" he asked. Chad nodded, already brimming with notes and ideas for improving neighborhood safety. As they drove back to the station, Chad reflected on his first real patrol lead. Bob patted his shoulder. "Clear communication, follow-through, respect—that's how you earn trust. Welcome to the force, Chad." Back at the station, Bob led Chad into the briefing room for their debrief. A whiteboard displayed key patrol points and feedback categories. Bob tapped the board. "Let's review your Willow Lane calls." Chad unrolled his notes. "Three residents reported speeding vehicles, stray dogs, and a broken streetlight. I documented each, coordinated with Animal Control for the dogs, and logged the streetlight issue with public works." Bob nodded, adding checkmarks beside each item. "Excellent documentation. Now, for speeding—what enforcement options did you consider?"

Chad glanced up. "I thought of increased patrol presence during morning drop-off, potential speed radar placement, and coordinating a community awareness campaign." Bob smiled broadly. "That's proactive thinking. Community engagement is as vital as citations. I'll support those recommendations." Bob then addressed de-escalation. "You remained calm, used clear language, and offered solutions—not just 'no' directives. That's how you build rapport."

Chad exhaled, relief evident. "Thank you. I've been practicing the techniques you showed me." Bob stood and retrieved two training certificates from the shelf. "One for completing your first solo-led patrol, and this one for community engagement excellence." He handed them to Chad. Chad accepted them, eyes bright. "I appreciate it, sir. I couldn't have done it without your guidance." Bob clapped him on the back. "You've earned it. Now, let's file your reports and then call it a day. Proud of what you've accomplished." Chad gathered his papers with a grin. As they walked out together, he felt confident stepping forward on his own—ready for the next untold adventure.

As the station emptied for the evening, Bob and Chad found themselves alone in the break room, the hum of the coffee maker the only sound. Chad poured two cups, handing one to Bob with a grateful nod. "Rookie's first big day," Chad said quietly, settling into a chair. "Couldn't have done it without your guidance." Bob accepted the cup and leaned back. "You did the work—you asked the right questions, stayed calm, and followed through. That's how good officers are made." Chad stared into his coffee. "I've been filling my notebook all day. I even sketched a quick diagram of the warehouse approach—and the proper leash technique with Scout." Bob smiled. "Good. Keeping records and sketches helps cement what you learn. I still refer to my old notes from my first week." Chad flipped open his notebook and showed Bob a page titled **"Lessons Learned – Day One"**, bullet points underlined:

- Maintain a safe angle during traffic stops

- Use clear, calm commands in confrontations

- Document every handoff in the evidence chain

- Engage the community with empathy

Bob tapped the page. "That's an excellent start. Add one more: 'Trust your instincts—but verify with training.'" Chad scribbled it in a red pen. They sat in companionable silence for a moment, the weight of the day settling into quiet pride. At last, Bob stood. "Rest up, Chad. Tomorrow we tackle emergency driving and med calls." Chad rose, a determined sparkle in his eyes. "Ready, sir." He closed his notebook and exhaled. "Thank you—for everything." Bob clapped him on the shoulder. "Tomorrow's adventure awaits. Get some sleep." The glow of dawn seeped through the break room window as Bob and Chad gathered their things. The station's corridors were silent, save for the distant hum of dispatch monitors. Bob clipped his radio to his belt and opened his notebook to a fresh page. "Time for your final reflection," he said, handing the pen to Chad.

Chad wrote in neat script:

> *"Day One: Understood that leadership isn't about orders—it's about guidance, patience, and trust. Officer Bob showed me the ropes, and I'm ready to pay it forward."*

He passed the notebook back. Bob read the entry and nodded with approval. "Well said. Keep writing those reflections—they'll chart your growth."

Chad grinned, pride shining in his eyes. Bob stood and stretched. "Alright, rookie—emergency driving training at 0800. See you in the yard." Chad saluted playfully. "Sir, yes, sir."

Bob headed toward his office, Scout trotting after him, while Chad slipped the notebook into his jacket pocket. As they parted ways, Bob thought of the countless officers he'd mentored over the years—and how the force's future depended on days like this. With one last look at the empty break room, Bob murmured, "Another story told."

Chapter 8: Community Flood Relief

The early morning sun glinted off the swollen riverbanks as Bob drove Scout to the town square. Barricades and sandbags lined the streets, and volunteers in bright vests shoveled mud and debris into wheelbarrows. The flood relief effort was in full swing. Bob stepped out of the cruiser and clipped Scout's leash to his belt. "Morning, everyone," he called, nodding to a half-dozen residents forming a human chain to pass sandbags. Their faces were streaked with sweat and determination.

Sarah, the volunteer coordinator, rushed over. "Officer Bob! Thank goodness you're here. We need help reinforcing the levee by the old mill." Bob glanced at Scout. The German Shepherd gave a soft bark, ready for action. "Lead the way," Bob said. He threaded his vest pockets with gloves, a small first-aid kit, and his radio. They followed a narrow street to the crumbling levee where water lapped at the grass. A dozen townspeople formed a line, handing sandbags down the embankment. Bob joined the chain, lifting heavy bags and passing them along with efficient precision. A shout went up: a section of the levee was starting to weep under the pressure. Bob raced forward, sliding onto his knees in the mud.

He pressed his gloved hand against the soft spot and barked instructions: "More bags here! Dig that trench deeper to direct the water away!" Volunteers redoubled their efforts, shovels clinking, boots squelching. Scout nosed the ground nearby, then stood guard as Bob directed traffic, countless passing cars slowing to rubberneck before yielding to the relief crew.

By mid-morning, the levee held firm. Hoses diverted overflowing water into sand-lined trenches, and Bob surveyed the work with relief. He wiped mud from his brow and addressed the group. "Great work, everyone—we just bought the town more time." He handed Sarah his radio. "Requesting dump trucks with more fill material and the county engineer for reinforcement plans." Sarah clicked her mic. "Copy that, Unit 14. They'll be here in twenty." Bob rose, brushing mud from his knees, and looked at Scout. "Let's keep at it. There's still a lot of ground to cover." Dump trucks rumbled up Main Street, their beds heavy with gravel and sand mix. Bob directed the first truck to the breached section while Scout patrolled the perimeter, alert for any oncoming vehicles. As the driver tipped the load, Bob joined Sarah and her team, spreading the material with shovels. The river's roar grew louder, but the new barrier held firm.

A volunteer called out that the county engineer, Mr. Patel had arrived with his clipboard. Bob jogged over. "Morning, Mr. Patel. Good to see you." Patel adjusted his hard hat. "I've run the numbers—this mix should withstand another foot of water rise. We'll layer it and compact it every ten feet." He handed Bob a diagram. "Follow these zones." Bob nodded and relayed the plan to the crew. They formed new chains, shovels dipping in rhythm under Patel's guidance. Children from a nearby shelter arrived, carrying buckets of small rocks to fill gaps. Bob knelt to thank them. "Every bit helps—great job!" Scout received grateful pats from the children before moving on to examine the far end of the levee. Bob followed, finding a small sinkhole forming under the pressure. He flagged down two volunteers and called for extra sandbags.

Working together, they filled the void and smoothed the surface. Bob offered words of encouragement: "Keep it steady—slow and even, just like training." The volunteers exchanged determined looks and redoubled their efforts. By noon, the sand-and-gravel barrier stretched uninterrupted along the creek. Mud-caked boots and glistening faces testified to hours of backbreaking work. Sarah approached Bob, handing him a bottle of water. "Thank you," she said. "We couldn't have done it without you."

Bob took a long drink, then surveyed the scene—volunteers packing up tools, engineers marking final inspections, and Scout wagging his tail in approval. He tapped his radio: "Unit 14 to command—levee reinforced, evacuation hold lifted. Returning to the station for debrief." A crackling reply came: "Copy that, Bob. Outstanding work." Bob shouldered his shovel one last time and patted Scout. "Let's get home, partner. Today's chapter is written." Back at the station later that afternoon, Bob hung his mud-splattered vest on the drying rack and joined the debrief in the briefing room. Volunteers from the fire department, engineering division, and city council were present, and a projector displayed before-and-after images of the levee.

Lieutenant Ramirez tapped the screen. "Officer Bob, your leadership was instrumental. Any takeaways for future flood responses?" Bob stood, brushing off residual grit. "First, early coordination with public works is crucial—having materials staged upstream saves time. Second, clear zone assignments kept volunteers organized. And third, engaging the community early—kids and local teams—boosted morale and manpower." A councilmember nodded appreciatively. "We'll incorporate your points into the new emergency plan."

After the meeting, Bob returned to his desk and opened his notebook:

Reflection:
When water threatened to overrun our town, unity was our greatest tool. Professional crews laid the groundwork, but neighbors brought heart.

He jotted one more note:

Action Items:

1. Coordinate pre-flood training with schools and community centers

2. Pre-position sandbag stations at key points

3. Schedule quarterly drills with all departments

Closing the notebook, Bob watched as Scout padded in, tail wagging. He scratched the dog's ears. "Good job today, buddy—another story added."

He powered down his computer and headed home, satisfied that his community was safer—and that the lessons of today would strengthen tomorrow's defenses. That evening, Bob stepped into the quiet of his home, still feeling the weight of the day's work. Sarah greeted him in the doorway, wiping her hands on a dish towel. "Dinner's waiting, but first—tell me about the levee." Bob removed his boots and sank onto the couch, Scout curling at his feet. He described the day: the sandbag chains, Patel's engineering plans, and even the children's eager help. Sarah listened, eyes bright. "So you really helped save the town," she said, setting a plate beside him. "That's… incredible." Bob shrugged, cheeks pink. "Just part of the job. But seeing everyone come together—that's what made it special." He ate quietly, replaying John's nod of approval during debrief, the volunteers' exhausted smiles, and Scout's enthusiastic barks. After dinner, he fetched his notebook from the jacket pocket and handed it to Sarah. "I wrote some reflections today," he said. She read aloud:

> *"Unity builds resilience. When we face rising waters, we rise together."*

Sarah smiled and hugged him. "Your words will inspire more than just officers."

Bob closed the notebook with care. "Let's hope so." Later, as the sun set, he filled one last journal entry for the chapter:

> *"Today proved that community is our greatest asset—stronger than any barrier we stack."*

He snapped it shut, glanced at Scout sleeping by the fireplace, and whispered, "Another story told." The next morning, Bob arrived early at the community center for a planning session with school principals and neighborhood association leaders. Scout padded at his side as tables were set with maps, markers, and printed flood-response guides.

Bob tapped the marker against the whiteboard. "Thank you all for coming. Today, we'll outline our pre-flood drill schedule and designate sandbag stations." He traced the river's path on the map. "We'll place stations at these key intersections: Cedar, Main, and Elm. Volunteers should know their primary pick-up point." A principal raised her hand. "Can we involve students in the drills?" she asked. Bob smiled. "Absolutely. I propose a safety fair beforehand—demonstrations by our K-9 unit, rope-tying workshops, and a mock rescue scenario. It'll teach kids valuable skills and build community resilience."

Scout sat patiently as Bob assigned roles: community leaders to coordinate volunteer teams, teachers to supervise student groups, and city staff to manage equipment. Each person took a printed schedule, nodding in agreement. As the meeting wrapped, a neighborhood rep handed Bob a folder. "We've drafted a flyer template. Can you review it?" Bob flipped through colorful designs showing Scout leading children in a drill. He nodded approvingly. "This is perfect. Let's distribute it to every household." Bob gathered the materials and stepped outside into the crisp morning air. He looked at Scout, leash in hand. "We're ready, buddy. Let's make sure our town knows what to do before the next flood."

Later that afternoon, Bob and Scout led the first flood drill at Cedar Elementary School. Bright cones marked "Safe Zone" and "Evacuation Route" along the playground. Students lined up eagerly, clutching laminated maps. Bob addressed the gathered crowd—children, parents, and teachers alike. "Today, we practiced what to do when the waters rise. Follow the arrows, stay calm, and help each other." He nodded to Scout, who sat obediently at his side, a demonstration in discipline.

The whistle blew, and the drill began. Students marched along the pre-designated path toward high ground near the football field. Bob guided smaller groups, offering praise: "Great job, Harriet—keep your eyes on the path!" Scouts marched alongside, a reassuring presence.

At the "Safe Zone," teachers checked attendance as Bob and school staff quizzed students on what to bring in an emergency kit. Backpacks opened to reveal water bottles, snack bars, and flashlights—proof the safety fair lessons had sunk in. After the drill, Bob gathered the participants. "Excellent work! Remember, practice makes you prepared." He handed out stickers shaped like sandbags and K-9 paws. Child after child reached for one, their smiles bright.

As the crowd dispersed, a teacher approached Bob. "Thank you for making safety fun—and memorable." Bob shrugged modestly. "If they know the drill, they'll stay safe." Scout wagged his tail in agreement. Bob packed up the cones and maps, the afternoon sun low in the sky. Another hurdle cleared—another community stronger for the effort. He ruffled Scout's ears and whispered, "Another story told." The late afternoon sky over the town square was streaked with gold as Bob returned the borrowed cones and maps to the supply shed.

Scout padded beside him, nose twitching at the scent of wet grass. Just as they were about to leave, Bob's radio crackled:

> "Unit 14, we have a call from Mrs. Alvarez on Pine Street—her basement's showing signs of seepage. Could use an officer's assistance."

Bob glanced at Scout. "One more stop, partner." They jogged to Mrs. Alvarez's tidy bungalow, where the elderly woman met them at the doorstep, worry etched on her face. "Officer Bob," she greeted softly. "Thank you for coming." She led them down a narrow staircase into a dim basement. Damp spots spread across the walls, and a slow trickle of water dripped into a plastic bin.

Bob knelt, inspecting the seepage line. "Your sump pump failed during the heavy rain—water's seeping just above its reservoir. I'll get Public Works to dispatch someone right away." He radioed dispatch: "Unit 14 to Public Works—sump pump failure at 24 Pine Street. Please expedite." Then he handed Mrs. Alvarez his business card. "If the water rises before they arrive, call me directly. I'll help move your valuables upstairs." Mrs. Alvarez's eyes brimmed with relief.

"You've been so kind." She squeezed his hand. "Thank you." Bob and Scout helped carry a few small boxes of family photos to the living room. Scout gently nudged a framed picture with his nose, as if sensing its importance. Bob smiled and patted the frame. "Safe and sound." As they left, Bob called back, "Stay safe, Mrs. Alvarez. Help is on the way." Outside, Scout sat obediently by the cruiser while Bob tapped his hat. "Every life matters—no story too small." He climbed in and started the engine, the sun dipping low as they headed back to the station—knowing the next chapter would be waiting.

Back at the station that evening, Bob washed the mud from his boots in the equipment bay while Scout received a thorough pat-down from the K-9 handler. The day's exercises had left both of them tired but satisfied. Bob climbed the stairs to the briefing room, where Lieutenant Ramirez and Sarah were reviewing today's drill metrics—participation rates, average evacuation times, and feedback comments. Sarah looked up and waved him over. "Bob, we've compiled the data," she said, handing him a summary sheet. "Drill efficiency improved by 40% compared to last year, and 95% of students knew their evacuation routes."

Bob studied the numbers. "Those are impressive," he said, smiling. "It shows the community's dedication—and that our pre-flood planning is working." Lieutenant Ramirez nodded. "We'll integrate this into the official emergency plan. I want you to lead the next review session with the City Council." Bob accepted the assignment with a nod. "Consider it done." He tapped the summary sheet. "Let's schedule quarterly drills and expand to nearby districts." Sarah added, "And we'll send out updated flyers using your draft template."

Bob placed the sheet in his notebook under a new tab: **Flood Relief Planning**. He closed it and shared a look with Scout, who wagged his tail as if in agreement. As the station lights dimmed for the night, Bob took a final walk past the evidence board—now decorated with before-and-after photos of the levee and smiling faces from the school drill. He paused, touching one photo of Scout guiding a child to safety. With a soft exhale, he whispered, "Another story told." The next morning, Bob arrived at the café for a quick debrief over coffee with Sarah and Mr. Patel. Scout waited patiently by the door. They sat at an outside table overlooking the now-quiet riverbank.

Sarah opened her tablet. "I've scheduled the next drill for three months from today. We'll rotate to Oak District." She tapped the screen. "City Council has approved funding for neighborhood sandbag stations and training kits." Mr. Patel sipped his espresso. "Engineering is marking new tether points along the levee. I'll share the updated blueprints with your team."

Bob nodded, jotting notes in his notebook:

Next Steps:

1. Drill at Oak District – September 14

2. Distribute 200 training kits to schools

3. Install tether posts at five critical spots

Their conversation paused as a local reporter approached, microphone in hand. "Officer Bob, can you comment on yesterday's drill success?" Bob straightened. "Our community showed incredible teamwork.

Preparedness saves lives, and today's numbers prove we're on the right track. We'll keep improving, one drill at a time." The reporter thanked him and left. Bob exchanged a glance with Sarah. "That'll help spread the word." After finishing their coffees, Bob rose and patted Scout's head. "Thanks for the meeting, team. Let's keep this momentum." As he walked back to his cruiser, Bob reflected on the chain of events—from sandbags and school drills to town-wide preparedness. Another flood season loomed, but now the community was stronger, ready for whatever came next. That evening, Bob returned to his office and placed the day's summary sheet into the "Flood Relief Planning" binder. He flipped to the cover and added a sticky note labeled "Chapter 8 Complete." Scout nosed the binder curiously, as if reading over his shoulder.

Bob opened his notebook to a fresh page and wrote:

> **Closing Reflection:**
> *Today proved that resilience isn't built by barriers alone, but by the hands and hearts of neighbors working side by side. Preparedness is a shared story—and together, we write the best chapters.*

He snapped the notebook shut and set it on his desk. Turning off his desk lamp, he glanced at the shelf where earlier binders stood—chapters of standoffs, chases, rescues, and community bonds. He whispered to the quiet office, "Another story told."

On the wall, the evidence board now held a small poster announcing the next flood drill in Oak District. Bob tapped the poster lightly and smiled. Tomorrow, he'd begin the Cold Case Revival—but for tonight, the community could rest a little safer, their bonds stronger than ever. He gathered his coat and Scout's leash, leading his partner out into the cool night air. As they walked toward home, the distant glow of streetlights guided them onward—ready for the next untold adventure.

Chapter 9: Cold Case Revival

The detective's desk lamp illuminated a dusty file folder marked **"Cold Case: Miller Disappearance, 1995."** Bob slid on his reading glasses and lifted the blue-inked cover. The station's archives smelled of old paper and ink—each file a frozen moment in time. He tapped the folder. **"Twenty-nine years,"** he muttered, flipping through brittle witness statements and faded photographs of a missing college student. Jane Miller's last sighting: leaving a late-night study session at the old town library.

Bob leaned back, recalling the look on Mrs. Miller's face when she'd requested the review—hope mingled with decades of grief. He set the folder aside and pressed his radio. "Chad, I'm opening a cold case—Miller Disappearance. I need you to pull up the original incident report, surveillance logs, and any lab results we have on file." Chad's voice crackled back: "On it, sir. Send everything to your terminal now." Bob drummed his fingers on the desk, eyes tracing the grain of the wood. He spotted a small whiteboard with the original lead: **"Possible sighting near Elmcrest Bridge."** He circled it with a dry-erase marker and grabbed a fresh notepad.

Moments later, Chad arrived with a stack of printouts. Bob sorted them meticulously—timeline, witness interviews, unexamined alibi gaps. His mind raced: What had been overlooked? Which tiny clue was waiting for rediscovery? He tapped a photograph of Jane walking toward the bridge, coat collar turned up against a chilly October wind. A note scrawled by Detective Harris read: "Suspect: unknown male, dark coat. No further leads." Bob closed his eyes for a heartbeat. **"Time to talk to Harris,"** he said aloud. He opened his phone contact list and scrolled down to **"Ret. Det. Frank Harris."** Standing, Bob grabbed his coat and slipped the Miller file under his arm. He clipped on his radio. "Chad, lock this file in Evidence Room B. I'm heading out to see Detective Harris—let's see if age has sharpened any memories." Scout followed at his heels as Bob stepped into the early morning light, the fresh case in hand and a renewed determination in his stride.

Bob pulled into the gravel driveway of Harris's modest bungalow just past dawn. He killed the cruiser's engine and approached the front door, Scout padding silently at his side. Bob raised a fist and knocked twice. The door creaked open to reveal Ret. Det. Frank Harris—graying hair, lined face, but eyes still sharp as ever. He offered a weary smile. "Bob. Didn't expect you so early."

"Morning, Frank," Bob said, extending the Miller file. "I'm reopening the Jane Miller case. Thought you might remember details worth revisiting." Harris nodded and stepped aside. "Come in. Coffee?" Bob followed into a cramped living room, walls lined with framed commendations and faded newspaper clippings. Scout settled by a worn armchair. Harris disappeared into the kitchen and returned with two steaming mugs. Bob accepted one. "Thanks. What do you recall about that night at Elmcrest Bridge?" Harris took a slow sip, brow furrowing. "It was colder than we thought—October chill.

Jane was headed home; her roommate saw her on campus security footage. After that, nothing happened until the next day when her bicycle was found under the bridge." Bob opened the file and pointed to a witness statement. "This guy, Mark Shelton, said he saw her speaking to someone in a dark coat. Did you ever track his alibi?" Harris set down his mug. "We tried. Shelton was too spooked to talk further—claimed the man warned him to stay silent. We lost him after that." He sighed. "I never liked how that went cold." Bob tapped his pen thoughtfully. "I'd like to follow up. Might be time Shelton tells us everything—if we approach him differently."

Harris studied Bob's face. "He still lives around here. I know I'm retired—but he respects me. I'll give him a call." Bob nodded. "Appreciate it. Any other loose ends? Unsent items? Photos you held back?" Harris shuffled papers on a side table. "There was this"—he handed Bob a Polaroid of Jane standing by the bridge guardrail, a second figure half-hidden behind a post. "Never developed the full frame. I thought it was too grainy." Bob examined the photo under the lamp's glow. The shape of a man's coat lapel was visible. "I'll have tech to enhance this. Thank you, Frank." Harris pushed back his chair. "Keep me in the loop, son. I want this solved as much as you do."

Bob clipped the Polaroid to his folder. "You'll be the first I call." He drained his mug and stood. "I'll let you rest." Outside, Bob loaded the file into his cruiser and patted Scout. "Let's find Mark Shelton next." Bob navigated back onto Main Street, the Miller file and Polaroid secured on the passenger seat. Scout rested his head on Bob's knee, alert. They turned onto Elmcrest Avenue, the route toward Shelton's last known address. "Shelton's on Pineview Drive," Bob said, consulting his GPS. "Let's see if retirement agrees with him." They arrived at a tidy bungalow with a faded "Welcome" mat. Bob rolled down the window. "Scout, stand by," he murmured, snapping on his badge lanyard.

He stepped out and approached the front door, knocking with measured calm. After a moment, the door cracked open. Mark Shelton, thinner and grayer than in his original statement photo, peered out. His eyes widened at the sight of Bob's uniform. "Officer... Bob? From the Miller case?" Bob offered a gentle smile. "Yes, Mark. I'd like to revisit your statement—what you saw that night." He held out the Polaroid. "May I come in?" Shelton hesitated, glancing at Scout. The German Shepherd sat quietly, tail low. With a weary nod, Shelton stepped aside. "Come in. I've kept busy with gardening. Coffee?" Bob followed inside, Scout slipping through the open door and settling by the hearth. The living room smelled of lavender and soil. Shelton disappeared into the kitchen and soon returned with two mugs.

Bob accepted one. "Thank you. Mark, I know that night was traumatic. I'd like to understand more about the man you saw with Jane." Shelton's hands trembled slightly as he wrapped his fingers around the mug. "I've thought about it every year since," he said in a low voice. "He was tall, broad-shouldered—wore a dark wool coat. He leaned close and spoke—just a few words—but I was frozen." Bob nodded. "What did he say?"

Shelton swallowed. "He said, 'Stay out of this.' That warning…it terrified me more than seeing her bicycle there." Bob leaned forward. "Did you recognize his voice? Anything distinctive?" Shelton shook his head. "No accent—just steady and cold. But afterward, I felt watched. I moved away from town for a while." Bob penciled notes. "I'll have the photo enhanced to see more of his features. In the meantime, can you recall where you walked after the bridge?" Shelton stared at his mug, then exhaled. "I headed straight home—too afraid to tell anyone. I regret that now." Bob closed his notebook gently. "This helps more than you know, Mark. I'll be in touch once we analyze the photo. Thank you for your courage." He stood, dropping a business card on the table. Scout rose and nudged Shelton's hand, offering comfort. Bob shook Shelton's hand and stepped outside, Scout padding beside him. As they headed back to the cruiser, Bob whispered, "One more piece falls into place." Back at the station, Bob uploaded the Polaroid to the department's enhancement software. He watched as digital filters sharpened the image, revealing more of the shadowed figure's broad shoulders and the glint of a ring on his left hand. He printed the enhanced copy and clipped it into the Miller file.

Chad looked over his shoulder. "That ring—wasn't there mention of a signet in the original report?" Bob nodded. "Good memory. The victim's roommate said Jane received a gift—a family heirloom ring—from someone she met that term." He tapped the photo. "This could be the same one." He flipped to Jane's personal effects inventory. A small velvet pouch had gone unexamined; inside was her grandmother's signet ring, engraved with a unique crest. Bob pulled the pouch from the evidence vault and examined the ring's crest under a desk lamp. "The same crest," he murmured, holding the ring and photo side by side. He circled the image of the ring in the enhanced printout. "Our suspect wore Jane's ring that night." Chad leaned in. "So he had it—either he took it or she gave it to him willingly." Bob closed his eyes for a moment, connecting dots. "Time to revisit her friends and that social circle—anyone who'd recognize the crest or object to its disappearance." He gathered the Miller file, the ring, and the enhanced photo. "Chad, compile a list of Jane's classmates from that semester and cross-reference with anyone who owned that crest. We'll start interviews tomorrow." Chad tapped his tablet. "On it, sir." Bob slipped the ring into an evidence bag, sealing it carefully. "This case is finally waking up." He straightened, determination shining in his eyes. "Let's find out who wore Jane's ring that night—and why."

The next morning, Bob convened in the conference room with Chad and Records Clerk Martinez. Stacks of yearbooks and class directories spread across the table. Bob tapped his pen against the Miller file. "All right," he said, voice steady. "Let's begin with Jane's roommate, Lisa Thornton. She was closest to Jane in those weeks. Chad, pull up her contact info. I'll call her." Chad nodded and swiped through his tablet. Bob dialed the number, listening as the line rang. "Lisa Thornton," came a tired voice. "Hello?" "Good morning, Ms. Thornton. This is Officer Bob with the Cold Case Unit. I'm re-examining Jane Miller's disappearance and would like to ask you a few questions. Is this a good time?" A soft sigh. "I—I've wondered if anyone would ever come back to this case. Yes, I'm available."

Bob jotted down a time for an in-person interview at the station. "Thank you. Please bring anything you still have from your shared apartment—notes, letters, anything that might help." Lisa agreed, and Bob hung up, pressing his palm to his notebook. "She's in tomorrow at 1100 hours." Chad looked up. "Next, we cross-reference classmates for that ring's crest. I pulled alumni records and found three students from the same fraternity whose family crests match. I've ranked them by proximity to Elmcrest Bridge."

Bob scanned the list. "Good work. We'll start with the fraternity president, Daniel Hewitt. I'll send him a formal interview request." He drafted an email on his laptop, summarizing the case's status and requesting Hewitt's voluntary cooperation. As he hit "Send," Scout padded in and nudged the Miller file. Bob smiled. "Thanks, partner. Let's hope this breaks it wide open." Outside the conference room, Bob paused to admire the enhanced Polaroid on the evidence board: the ring, the coat lapel, the half-hidden silhouette. For the first time in decades, the pieces were aligning.

Bob spent the afternoon reviewing Daniel Hewitt's background. The fraternity president had graduated top of his class and was known for community service—including a fundraiser at the Elmcrest Bridge walkway years ago. Bob flagged that event for follow-up. At 3:00 PM, Chad announced, "Ms. Thornton is here," as Lisa Thornton entered the interview room, clutching a small box. Bob offered her water and gestured to a chair. "Thank you for coming in," he began gently. "You brought something?" Lisa opened the box to reveal folded letters and journal pages. "Jane wrote these when she was stressed about finals. I thought they might help." She handed them over carefully.

Bob scanned the pages—entries about late-night walks, mentions of feeling watched, and one reference to a secret meeting "by the river's edge." He looked up. "Did she ever say who she was meeting?" Lisa hesitated. "She said she couldn't tell me at the time… but she trusted someone with her grandmother's ring. She called him 'C.' That's it."

Bob pressed a finger to his notebook. "C… could stand for several names, but it's a vital clue. Thank you, Ms. Thornton. We may call you again." As she left, Bob spoke quietly to Chad: "'C' and the ring crest—maybe a classmate's first initial. Let's add that to the list." Chad typed rapidly.

Next, Bob drafted a formal notice to Daniel Hewitt, setting an appointment for the following morning. He placed the Miller file back on his desk and leaned back. Scout tapped Bob's knee with his nose. Bob smiled and scratched Scout's ears. "We're closing in, buddy. Tomorrow we meet 'C'… and Daniel Hewitt."

The next morning, Bob and Chad parked outside Hewitt Hall on campus. The stone columns loomed overhead as they entered the administrative offices. Bob showed his badge and appointment letter; an assistant led them down to a polished conference room where Daniel Hewitt waited, poised in a tailored suit.

"Detective Bob," Hewitt greeted, voice measured. "I appreciate your discretion on this matter." Bob nodded and sat. "Mr. Hewitt, thank you for meeting with us. I'd like to discuss your involvement with Ms. Miller around the time of her disappearance." He placed the Polaroid on the table, the enhanced ring image facing Hewitt. Hewitt's eyes flicked to the photo. "I recognize that ring—it belonged to Jane. She gifted it to me during our senior year... as a thank-you for helping her campaign for student government." Chad leaned forward. "Campaign—in this photo, you were wearing that coat the night she vanished?" Hewitt's jaw tightened. "Yes. I picked her up after her study group at the library and walked her to the bridge to meet a fellow campaign volunteer. I left before she did." His gaze softened. "I never saw her again."

Bob tapped a notepad. "You left her at the bridge—around 10:45 PM?" Hewitt nodded solemnly. "She wanted to discuss polling, then she reached into her pocket and showed me the ring—said she felt safe giving it to me." He paused. "I wore it home, then returned it the next day... but I never saw the gift pouch in her belongings when the investigation began." Bob exchanged a look with Chad. "That pouch came from her apartment—found with her grandmother's ring missing. If you returned it, it must have been removed before inventory." Hewitt swallowed. "I… I may have handed it off to someone else later that night. She asked me to give it to her roommate for safekeeping. I never confirmed it was returned to her." Bob scribbled a note. "Thank you for your honesty. We'll need that detail on record."

He reached into an evidence bag and withdrew the ring. "This is the pouch and ring as found in evidence—could be the key to tracing custody beyond you." Hewitt looked away, regret in his eyes. "I understand. I want justice for Jane, Detective." Bob rose, closing the case folder. "We'll continue following every lead. Thank you for your cooperation." Outside the campus building, Bob paused, closing his notebook. "Chad, this changes our timeline—someone else handled that pouch."

Chad nodded. "We'll add it to our suspect matrix." Bob patted Scout. "Onward—time to meet 'C' and uncover who that someone else was." Back at the precinct, Bob and Chad spread the updated suspect matrix across the conference table. Each column tracked initials, ring custody, and known whereabouts. A bold "C" sat next to Caldwell, Carter, and Chambers.

Chad pointed to the first entry. "Chris Caldwell was in that campaign, too—a close friend of Hewitt's. He's now a local businessman. I've got his contact info." Bob nodded. "Let's start there." He punched in the number. After two rings, a voice answered, "Hello?" "Mr. Caldwell?" Bob identified himself and arranged a brief meeting at the station. Within the hour, Chris Caldwell—mid-thirties, neatly dressed—entered the interview room, nerves flickering behind polite eyes.

Bob opened the file. "Chris, Jane Miller entrusted you with her grandmother's ring that night. We know Hewitt passed it to you. Can you confirm?" Caldwell swallowed. "Yes. Daniel asked me to hold it until he could return it to Lisa Thornton the next day. I never delivered it—I kept it on my desk." He exhaled. "I was going to surprise Jane with it at the campaign gala—but then… she disappeared."

Bob leaned in. "Where is that desk now?" Caldwell hesitated, then nodded. "It's at my law office. I can bring it in." Within two hours, Bob stood in Caldwell's office as the desk was opened. Hidden in a drawer lay the velvet pouch—now yellowed with age—and the missing ring. Bob bagged the pouch as evidence. "Thank you for coming forward. This is pivotal." He looked at Chad. "Next step: lab analysis on the pouch—any hair fibers, fingerprints, anything."

Caldwell nodded, relief and guilt mingling on his face. "I'm so sorry this stayed hidden." Bob closed his notebook. "We'll follow the forensic results. You'll hear from us again." As they left Caldwell's office, Scout trotted behind the cruiser. Bob patted his partner's flank. "Another piece found—a cold case is heating up." Back at the lab, Bob and Chad watched as forensic technician Lopez swabbed the pouch interior. Under bright lights, the fibers and latent prints would be catalogued and cross-checked against the department database.

Lopez looked up. "Preliminary fiber match: the fleece matches the lining of Jane's coat. Fingerprints are partial but may yield a usable profile." She labeled the swabs and set them aside. "I'll expedite the analysis." Bob nodded. "Thank you. Keep us posted." They left the lab and returned to the conference room, where the suspect matrix awaited. Chad exhaled. "So the pouch was in Caldwell's hands, but the fibers suggest it returned to Jane—then came back here. That implies Jane handed it off again, or someone retrieved it from her coat." Bob tapped a photo of the original crime scene. "In the shed, they recovered her hoodie with fibers—but no pouch. The pouch must have been separated prior to the shed." He circled "Shelton" and "Caldwell" on the matrix.

"Let's re-examine Shelton's statement—he saw her then. Could he have taken the pouch before running?" Chad pulled up Shelton's transcript. "He said he fled immediately after the warning. No mention of the pouch." Bob leaned back. "Let's get Shelton back in—gently. Ask if he noticed her coat pockets or anything she held." He rose. "I'll make the call." Chad nodded and began drafting the interview request. Bob patted Scout's head. "One more outreach. We're closing in." Late that afternoon, Shelton sat across from Bob in the interview room, fidgeting with the edge of his sleeve. Bob set the Polaroid on the table and spoke softly. "Mark, thank you for coming in again. I have a few more questions about the night you saw Jane." Shelton nodded, voice shaky. "I… I'll help any way I can." Bob studied Shelton's hands. "You saw Jane hand something to that man in the photo—the ring pouch, perhaps? Or did you notice anything else—keys, a bag?" Shelton's eyes darted away. He swallowed. "She had a small package… I thought it was her notes. It fell when she turned—green wrapping with a ribbon." He looked at the pouch in the evidence bag. "That's the one."

Bob leaned forward. "Did you pick it up?"
Shelton's shoulders slumped. "I did. I thought it was trash—soaked and muddy. I picked it up and… walked off. I panicked and kept it."

Bob nodded gently. "That explains the fibers matching your coat on the pouch. Thank you for telling the truth." Shelton's voice trembled. "I'm sorry. I never meant to hide anything." Bob closed his notebook. "Your honesty helps us rebuild the timeline. You may go now, but I'll be in touch."

As Shelton left, Bob examined the pouch again. "So she dropped it, you picked it up, and then… someone else must have gotten it after you?" Chad spoke from the doorway: "Pouch fibers also match someone else's jacket we found in the evidence vault—Detective Harris's old coat."

Bob's eyes widened. "That's our lead—Harris returned the pouch after collecting it from Shelton." He gathered the file. "Frank Harris, one more chat." Scout wagged in agreement as they headed out. The cold case's final piece was within reach.

Chapter 10: Lost Service Dog

The dawn air was crisp as Bob clipped Scout's leash to his belt and headed out to meet Officer Reyes at the K-9 unit kennel. Scout bounded ahead, tail wagging, eager for today's mission. Reyes greeted them with a clipboard in hand. "Morning, Bob. We've got a missing service dog—K-9 Scout's partner, Max—lost during a search at Pine Ridge Woods last night." Her brow was furrowed. "He slipped his harness after chasing a scent." Bob's heart tightened. "Max is trained to find missing elders with dementia. We need to get him back fast." He patted Scout reassuringly. "Let's gear up."

They loaded into the K-9 SUV, equipment rattling in the back: extra leashes, water, and Max's tracking vest, labeled in bold letters. Reyes handed Bob a handheld GPS beacon transmitter. "Max's vest beacon should still ping—range of about two miles." Bob clicked on the receiver. A faint beep answered, steady but weak. "Signal's coming from the northwest corner of the woods." He guided the SUV toward the trailhead, Scout's ears perked in anticipation. At the forest's edge, they donned high-visibility vests and gloves. Bob checked the transmitter again. "The signal's strongest near that stand of pines," he said, pointing.

Reyes released Scout. "Let's see if your partner can pick up Max's trail." Scout lifted his nose, scenting the morning breeze, then bolted toward the trees. Bob and Reyes followed, alert for any sign of the lost dog. Branches crackled underfoot as they pressed deeper. Bob glanced at the beacon: the signal's pulse quickened. "He's close." A low bark echoed ahead. Scout paused, ears raised. Bob exchanged a glance with Reyes: "There he is."

Through a thicket, Max appeared—standing atop a fallen log, tail wagging but eyes wary. His vest was torn and muddy, but he was unharmed. Bob let out a relieved breath. "Good boy, Max," he called softly. Scout bounded forward, nuzzling his canine comrade in greeting. Reyes approached and gently secured Max's leash. "You found him," she said, eyes moist. "Thank you, both of you."

Bob knelt to inspect Max's vest. "Let's get you home." He tapped the beacon off, and together they led the pair back toward the trailhead, hearts light with rescue accomplished. They emerged from the woods into the soft glow of morning, Scout and Max side by side, leashes held firmly by Bob and Reyes. At the trailhead parking lot, volunteers and paramedics had gathered, relief flooding their faces as they spotted the two dogs.

Bob handed Max's leash to a waiting volunteer. "He's safe now—just needs a quick check." Reyes knelt beside Max, gently running her hands along his legs and back. "No injuries," she reported after a careful exam. "He's a bit shaken and thirsty, but otherwise fine." A paramedic approached with a bowl of water and a towel. Bob guided Max toward it. The service dog lapped gratefully, tail wagging in slow circles. Bob patted his head. "Good job, buddy." Scout nudged Max playfully, and the two canines touched noses—a silent celebration of reunion. Bob exchanged a smile with Reyes.

"Thanks for coordinating the beacon gear," he said. "Couldn't have done it without that transmitter." Reyes stood, brushing leaves from her uniform. "Your tracking training helped too. Scout didn't falter." She ruffled Scout's ears. "You're quite the hero."

Bob led the group back toward the K-9 SUV. "Let's get Max to the vet station for a full check-up and then back to the handler's care." He opened the rear door, and both dogs climbed in, Scout padding in first, then Max settling beside him. As they drove back, Bob glanced in the rearview mirror at Scout and Max resting together, safe and content. He opened his notebook and jotted:

Reflection:
Two partners lost and found—reminder that every team relies on trust and training. Scout and Max bring hope to others; it's our duty to do the same.

He closed the notebook, feeling gratitude for the successful rescue. Ahead lay paperwork and congratulations, but for now, Bob savored the simple joy of two loyal dogs reunited and ready for their next call. Back at the station, Bob hung up Max's tracking vest to dry and led Scout to the small K-9 debrief room. Reyes joined them, carrying a clipboard. "Excellent work, both of you," Reyes said, checking her notes. "Max's vitals are stable, and his handler will be here shortly. I'll file the medical report." Bob knelt beside Scout, praising him softly. Scout's tail thumped against the floor. "Couldn't have done it without you," Bob murmured. Reyes tapped her pen against the clipboard. "We should run a quick training drill—simulate a similar scenario so Scout's ready next time." Bob nodded. "Agreed. Let's schedule it for tomorrow morning." He opened his notebook:

Training Note:
Live-search drill in Pine Ridge Woods at first light. Incorporate beacon failures and scent diversions.

He snapped the notebook shut and stood. "Time to check in with Max's handler and wrap up paperwork." They exited into the corridor, canine partners trailing behind, ready for whatever the day would bring next. The following morning, before sunrise, Bob and Reyes met at the trailhead of Pine Ridge Woods. Scout wore his harness once more, and nearby lay a spare tracking beacon wired to simulate a malfunction. Bob checked his watch—5:45 AM—and nodded to Reyes. "Beacon will be cut out at the first waypoint," she explained. "Then it's on Scout's nose to pick up the scent." Bob crouched beside Scout. "Remember: low voice, clear commands. Let him lead. I'll follow at a distance." Scout gave a crisp bark and dashed into the dim undergrowth, nose low to the leaf-strewn path.

They followed, flashlights bobbing. At the first marker stake, the beacon's light flickered off—simulated failure. Scout paused, then sniffed the air and bolted toward a cluster of fallen pine boughs. Bob jogged to keep pace, heart pounding with excitement. Scout nosed under the needles and emerged beside a camouflaged harness lying on the ground. He sat and looked back at Bob, tail wagging. Bob knelt to examine the harness—exactly where Max's had fallen.

He clipped a training dummy to Scout's pack as a reward and petted his partner. Reyes snapped a photo. "Signal back online in five seconds," she called. True enough, the beacon beeped, and Scout barked twice in approval. Bob rose, brushing dirt from his knees. "Exceptional work, Scout. Ready for the next challenge?" Scout barked and trotted forward, eager for more. Bob turned to Reyes, smiling in the dawn light. "This drill will keep our K-9 teams sharp. Max and Scout will both be safer next time." Together, they retraced their steps out of the woods—two handlers and two dogs, bonded by training, trust, and the shared goal of keeping their community safe.

Later that afternoon, Bob returned to the station's K-9 office to review the drill footage with Reyes. They watched as Scout navigated the simulated failure flawlessly, pinpointing the harness within minutes. Reyes paused the video and turned to Bob. "His response time was under three minutes," she noted. "That's faster than the last official test." Bob nodded, impressed. "He's improving—our training adjustments are paying off." He opened his notebook to a new entry:

After-Action Review:

1. Beacon failure simulation effective—Scout relied on scent, not tech.

2. Handler distance maintained—allowed Scout to lead without interference.

3. Recording the drill helps identify scent focus points for further refinement.

He closed the notebook and turned off the monitor. "Let's present this to the K-9 unit tomorrow—encourage all teams to adopt the malfunction drill." Reyes smiled. "Agreed. Max will benefit too when he's back on duty." Scout padded over, nosing Bob's hand, reminding him of the day's success. Bob knelt and scratched him behind the ears. "Good work, partner. Another story told—another skill honed." With the drill complete and Max safe, Bob felt the chapter draw to a close. He clipped his notebook to his belt and headed home, Scout trotting faithfully by his side—ready for the next untold adventure.

Chapter 11: Dispatch Drama

The crisp hum of the dispatch center greeted Bob as he stepped inside, Scout padding quietly at his heels. Rows of console screens glowed with incoming calls. Officer Lynn waved him over. "Morning, Bob. You're just in time—dispatch's been flooded with radio traffic tonight," she said, eyes on her monitor. "We lost the primary channel for a while." Bob glanced at the scrolling call log. "Let's see what happened." He moved to Lynn's station and peered at the waveform—a solid block of static had overridden several calls. The timestamp read 0215 hours.

Lynn tapped the mic. "Someone jammed our frequency—deliberate interference. I'm rerouting to backup channels, but it's slowing response times." Bob frowned. "We need to restore the main channel—and find who's causing the jam." He clipped his radio to his belt. "Chad, get me the tech team's lead. I'm heading to the communications tower." Back at the station's entrance, Bob and Scout hopped into the cruiser. Dispatch patched him through. "Bob to CommTech—what's the status?" A calm voice replied, "We've located the source near the old water treatment plant. I'll forward the coordinates."

Bob set his GPS and flipped on the lights. "Heading there now." As they pulled onto the road, the gravity of a compromised dispatch channel weighed on him—this was more than a nuisance; it was a threat to every call for help. Bob and Scout arrived at the rusted chain-link fence surrounding the water treatment plant. A lone figure crouched beside the satellite dish, fiddling with cables. Bob killed the engine and slipped out, badge in hand. "Police!" he called. "Step away from the equipment!"

The figure froze, helmet obscuring the face. A burst of static crackled through Bob's radio as the jammer activated again. Scout growled low, nose twitching in the damp grass. Bob drew his flashlight and beam-rested it on the suspect's hands—tool kit open, wires stripped. "Hands where I can see them," he commanded. The suspect rose slowly, revealing a teenage boy—eyes wide with remorse. Bob holstered his light. "I'm Officer Bob. You're interfering with emergency channels. Why?"

The boy's voice shook. "They never answered my call—they all ignored me. I just wanted them to hear me." He swallowed. "I'm sorry." Bob kept his tone calm. "Which channel did you jam on?" He nodded toward the dish. "Undo what you've done."

The teen hesitated, then reached for the wires. Under Bob's watchful eye, he reconnected the feed. Static hissed once, then cleared—the dispatch channel returned. Bob radioed dispatch: "Channel Clear—call signs back to normal." A crisp "Copy that" crackled in reply. Bob approached and placed a hand on the boy's shoulder. "People rely on these frequencies in life-or-death situations." He sighed. "Let's get you some help. You'll come with me—no jail time if you cooperate."

Scout licked the boy's hand, offering comfort. The teen nodded, tears in his eyes. Bob guided him toward the cruiser. "Everything will be okay," he promised. Bob secured the teenager in the back of his cruiser just as another patrol car pulled up with its lights off. Officer John stepped out, uniform crisp, smile broad. Bob hadn't seen his partner in weeks. "John?" Bob blinked. "You're back—welcome back!" John opened the passenger door and leaned in. "Just got off paternity leave. Baby Evan's already three months old—Mom and I are doing great. Figured the precinct needed me back." He offered Bob a small photo of his son, swaddled and sleeping. Bob slipped the photo into his breast pocket. "He's perfect. Congratulations, brother." John clipped on his radio and tapped the jammer's control unit beside the dish. "I've isolated the interference circuits—looks like our teen used low-grade components. I'll haul this back for analysis." He handed a set of cuffs to Bob. "I'll drive him in, clear the tech team to sweep frequencies, and get dispatch fully online." Bob nodded. "Couldn't ask for a steadier hand." He patted the teen's shoulder through the cage. "You're coming with us—let's get you warmed up and talk this out."

John guided the suspect into his cruiser while Bob radioed dispatch: "Unit 18 – channel secure, suspect in custody. Send me your best tech officer." A crisp "Copy that" crackled. As John's cruiser pulled away, Bob turned to Scout. "Good to have you back, partner," he whispered, scratching Scout's ears. Then he strode toward the comms tower with renewed confidence—knowing that whatever came next, he wouldn't face it alone. Bob climbed the rusted stairs of the communications tower alongside CommTech lead Engineer Diaz, while John coordinated at the base. The wind whipped at their coats as static crackled again—brief, but enough to jeopardize an emergency call. Diaz pointed to a battered jammer device tied to the tower's coaxial line. "It's rudimentary—probably scavenged parts. I'll cut power to the line and secure the rig." He set to work with a wirecutter.

John's voice crackled over Bob's radio. "Bob, dispatch is back online. They're moving all sensitive traffic to the encrypted backup channel as we speak." Bob relayed to Diaz: "Once you've removed the jammer, lock this piece of equipment up. I'll file for warrants." With a final snip, the device clattered to the rooftop. The tower's main receiver hummed back to life, clean and steady. Bob tapped his mic: "Unit 14 and 18—frequency clear. Great work team." Below, John signaled the tech crew to pack up. He jogged up the stairs to join them, cradling a sleepy three-month-old Evan in one arm, baby monitor clipped to his belt. Scout's excited bark echoed through the tower's hatch.

Bob's eyes widened. "John—and Evan! Didn't expect guests up here." John grinned, offering Bob a quick family snapshot. "Couldn't miss the big bust. Daddy's bringing home the bad guy—and his kid." He patted Evan's back gently as the baby cooed. Bob smiled. "Congratulations again, brother. Ready to head back?" Diaz secured the jammer in an evidence bag. John threaded the straps on his infant carrier. Together, they descended, the sun cresting the horizon—dispatch secure, family present, and another crisis averted.

Back at the precinct, the morning's first light filtered through the windows as Bob, John, and Engineer Diaz convened in the briefing room. Dispatch consoles hummed steadily, their screens free of static. Lieutenant Ramirez addressed the group. "Great job restoring the channel and securing that jammer. CommTech has confiscated the device, and we've routed all emergency traffic to the encrypted backup until further notice."

Diaz nodded. "We'll analyze the components and trace where the parts came from. That should help identify any accomplices." John glanced down at Evan, snug in his carrier. The baby stirred, yawning. "Looks like I'm back to juggling two calls—fatherhood and patrol," he quipped. Bob chuckled. Bob turned to Diaz. "Keep me posted on your findings. In the meantime, we'll run extra patrols around critical infrastructure—towers, power substations—to deter copycats." Ramirez thanked them all. As the meeting adjourned, Bob patted John's shoulder. "Glad to have you back, partner. And congrats again on Evan." John smiled, handing the baby to Bob for a quick handful of cuddles. "Thanks. Appreciate the backup—both on duty and off." Scout barked softly, as if in agreement. Outside, the first normal 911 call crackled in, and Bob answered: "Unit 14, what's your emergency?" With dispatch restored, life—and duty—returned to its steady rhythm.

With dispatch fully operational, Bob and John climbed into their respective cruisers—Bob in Unit 14, John in Unit 18—ready to patrol the zones around critical city infrastructure. Scout settled in the front seat of Bob's car, ears perked for any unusual sounds. "Let's make sure no one tries a stunt like that again," Bob said, pulling into the downtown district. John's voice came over the radio: "Copy that, Bob. I'll run to the north side. Meet you at the substation in thirty." Bob eased onto Main Street, scanning rooftops and alleyways. He checked his mirror: Scout's eyes stayed fixed on the road, always watchful. As they passed the water treatment plant, Bob nodded to John, who gave a thumbs-up from his cruiser. Halfway to the power substation, Bob's radio crackled:

> "Unit 14, we have reports of suspicious activity near the old radio tower—two figures carrying a ladder after hours."

Bob responded immediately: "On it." He flicked on the lights and headed toward Maple Avenue, Scout alert at his side. He arrived to find two teens whispering as they hoisted the ladder against the locked fence. Bob cut the engine and approached, voice firm: "Police—step away from that ladder!"

The pair froze, then dropped the ladder and raised their hands. Bob called in: "Unit 14 to dispatch—two in custody for attempted trespass at radio tower. Please send a patrol wagon." Within minutes, John pulled up. "Need assistance?" he asked, stepping out. Bob nodded. "Just crowd control." Together they frisked the teens, secured the ladder as evidence, and guided them to the patrol wagon.

John glanced at Scout, who sat obediently by the fence. "Nice work," he said. "No one's messing with our channels tonight." Bob smiled and patted Scout. "Couldn't have done it without you—and my best backup." He handed the ladder off to arriving officers. As the teens were led away, Bob and John exchanged a look of relief: another potential jammer thwarted, another night's calm restored.

With the two teens secured in the back of the patrol wagon, Bob and John walked a perimeter check around the radio tower fence. The night air was crisp, and the tower's beacon blinked steadily above them. John shrugged off his jacket and draped it over the fence. "My shift ends soon. I'll file the trespass report, then I'm off to catch up on dad duty—Evan's first pajama party tonight." Bob grinned. "Sounds like a good gig. I'll clear the scene and finish the tech liaison.

Then I'll call it a night, too." John patted the fence rail. "Thanks for having my back—and Scout's." He stepped back into Unit 18 and gave Scout a friendly rub as the K-9 wolfhound peered through the fence. Bob watched as John climbed in, then swept the area one last time with Scout's keen eyes—nothing out of place. He called dispatch: "Unit 14 clear. No further threats detected. You can stand down the additional patrols." A satisfied "Copy that" came through. Bob climbed back into his cruiser, Scout curling in the passenger seat. He closed the night's log on his tablet:

Dispatch Drama Wrap-Up:

- Jammer device secured and passed to CommTech

- Extra patrols thwarted potential copycat

- Dispatch channel restored without interruption

He saved the entry and shut off the screen. Outside, the city slept peacefully under the restored radio waves. Bob patted Scout's flank. "Another crisis managed—and another story told."

The next morning, Bob arrived at the dispatch center just as Lynn was wrapping up the overnight shift debrief. He slipped into a chair beside her console. "Morning, Bob," Lynn greeted. "We ran test transmissions all night—no more interference." She waved a printout. "Channels stable, logs clear."

Bob exhaled. "That's a relief. Dispatch can't afford downtime." He glanced down the hall toward the conference room. "How's John holding up with Evan?" Lynn smiled. "He's doing great. He brought Evan in yesterday—everyone got a chance to coo over him." Bob chuckled. "He's a natural dad. I owe him lunch—thanks for covering while I handled the tower." Lynn tapped her headset off. "I'll join you—I need a break from screens."

They headed to the precinct café, Scout padding at Bob's heels. Over sandwiches, they recounted the week's chaos: jammers, patrols, and crisis averted. As Bob stood to leave, he checked his watch. "Time to file final reports and then swing by John's to welcome him fully back." He ruffled Scout's ears. "Another story told—and another friend moment ahead." With dispatch secure and their partnership stronger than ever, Bob and Lynn walked out into the morning sun—ready for whatever new chapter lay beyond the horizon.

That afternoon, Bob settled at his desk to draft the official after-action report. He opened a fresh document template and began:

> **Incident:** Unauthorized jammer device at Water Treatment Plant tower
> **Date/Time:** June 7, 2025, 0215–0400 hours
> **Units Involved:** 14 (Bob), 18 (John), CommTech, Dispatch
> **Outcome:** Device secured; dispatch channel restored; two suspects arrested for trespass attempts

He paused, then added a personal note in his field notebook:

> *"John's return—and seeing him balance patrol and fatherhood—reminded me that our work supports families as much as communities."*

He printed the report and routed it to Lieutenant Ramirez, then packed up his badge and logbooks. Outside his office, the trophy case reflected the afternoon sun—a testament to decades of service. Bob ran a finger along the glass.

"Another story preserved," he murmured, tucking the after-action printout into the case folder. As the sun dipped low, Bob grabbed his coat and Scout's leash. He drove to John's home one last time for the evening. The bungalow glowed warmly, and through the window he saw John reading bedtime stories to little Evan.

Bob parked quietly and slipped inside. John looked up, relief and surprise on his face. "Hey—didn't think you'd show up again." Bob knelt beside the sofa and offered a small book of bedtime rhymes. "Scout and I brought a story for Evan." The baby gurgled, reaching for the colorful cover. John smiled, standing to let Bob tuck the book into Evan's chubby hands. "Perfect timing. Ready for the next chapter, buddy?" Bob ruffled Evan's hair gently. "Always." He stood and clasped John's shoulder. "Good work out there—and at home." Scout wagged beside them.

John nodded. "Couldn't have done it without you." As the trio shared a quiet moment, Bob reflected on how every case—from jammers to rescues—wove into their lives and families. He stepped outside into the fading light, Scout close behind, and whispered to the night air: "Another story told."

Chapter 12: Undercover at the County Fair

Twilight lanterns swayed above the fairgrounds as carnival music drifted on warm evening air. Bob stood near the entrance in plain clothes—jeans, a baseball cap, and mirrored sunglasses—blending into the crowd. Scout, fitted with a special K-9 vest, sat alert by his side. Across the midway, John waited beside a food stand, flipping a funnel cake in secret service uniform. A badge tucked inside his jacket confirmed his cover. He caught Bob's eye and gave a subtle nod: the meeting was on. Bob clipped a small radio mic to his collar. "All set?" he murmured. John nodded. "Fair's packed—good spot for pickpockets and purse snatchers. Let's split up: I'll start near the Ferris wheel, you check the game row." He handed Bob a carnival map marked "hot zones." Bob accepted it and tucked it into his pocket. "Got it. We'll reconvene in thirty minutes by the livestock tents." He patted Scout's harness. "Ready, partner?" Scout barked softly and slipped off-leash into the crowd, nose down, scanning for scents. Bob followed, weaving past children chasing spinning teacups and couples sharing cotton candy. At the dart-throw game, Bob watched a young man lean too close to a woman's purse dangling on her shoulder. Scout angled in, silently guiding Bob forward. Just as the thief's hand dipped for the wallet, Scout's low growl froze him in place.

Bob stepped out. "Evening, sir—hands where I can see them." The man stammered, dropping the wallet. Bob retrieved it and handed it back to the startled woman. Across the midway, John intercepted a trio of teenagers craning their necks over a prize wall. One fumbled a stolen plush toy toward his pocket as John cleared his throat. The teens jumped, then sheepishly returned the toy.

John flashed his badge. "Let's keep the prizes on the stands, folks." He nodded to Bob across the fair, who gave an approving thumbs-up. Scout rejoined Bob, tail wagging. Bob crouched to scratch behind his ears. "That's two down. Let's keep sweeping."

He checked his watch: twenty minutes left before regrouping. The county fair's lights glowed brighter, but with Scout at his side—and John watching the shadows—tonight's undercover operation was off to a strong start. Bob moved away from the dart booth, following Scout's steady pace toward the ring-toss alley. The clink of glass bottles and cheerful shouts masked herding crowds, but Scout honed in on a faint scent—a telltale whiff of recently handled cash and tissues. They reached a small cluster of midway workers counting their nightly earnings. One attendant's gloved hand hovered over a wad of bills in his apron pocket. Scout pressed close, tail low, signaling Bob.

Bob cleared his throat. "Excuse me—routine check." He tapped the man's shoulder. "May I see your permit and your cash reconciliation sheet?" The worker stiffened, nervously shuffling the bills. He handed Bob a wrinkled permit but balked at the request for the sheet. Bob's calm but firm tone left no room for argument. "Company policy—must be verified. Now." Hands trembling, the attendant produced a ledger showing payouts and ticket sales. Bob scanned the entries—one night's coverage clearly noted. He looked up. "That extra hundred goes in the till, not your pocket." The attendant's eyes widened with panic. Bob produced his badge subtly. "Step away from the booth. I'll handle things from here." He signaled Scout to stay back.

Meanwhile, across the midway, John crouched behind a game stand, watching a pickpocket lift a phone from a distracted teenager. John sprang into action, grabbing the suspect's wrist in one fluid motion. "Purse snatchers don't fare well here." He cuffed the teen on the spot. A stunned crowd erupted in applause. John led the youth toward the security gate, badge gleaming beneath the carnival lights. Bob rejoined him with the detained booth attendant in tow. "Looks like we've cleaned up more than just games tonight," Bob said quietly. He clipped a pair of evidence tags to the seized cash.

John nodded, satisfied. "Let's finish up and meet by the livestock tents—time for the big finale." Bob and John slipped through the crowd toward the livestock tents, where fairgoers gathered to watch the sheep-shearing demonstration. The festive chatter was laced with the bray of goats and the lowing of cattle. Lanterns strung between poles cast a warm glow over the pens. "Keep an eye out for any unusual activity," Bob murmured to John as they approached. Scout padded ahead, nose to the ground.

John scanned the perimeter. "Looks calm—but that crowd is ripe for pickpockets regrouping." He tipped his cap, then spotted a man slipping away from the tent entrance with a suspicious bulge in his jacket. Bob caught the movement and nodded. "Scout, trailer!" he whispered. Scout bounded forward, intercepting the man as he ducked behind a hay bale. "Evening," Bob called, stepping out. "Mind if I check your coat?" The man froze, then slowly raised his hands. John stepped up, easing a set of handcuffs into position. Bob patted the man down, removing a wallet stuffed with IDs not his own. "Looks like you've been busy." He snapped the wallet into an evidence pouch. Nearby, the sheep shearer paused mid-cut, watching in surprise. Fairgoers muttered as the suspect was led away.

John turned to Bob. "Two from the midway, two from the games—quite the haul tonight." Bob tucked the wallet into his pocket. "Night's not over yet. Let's sweep the surrounding tents before we call it a wrap." He checked his watch. "Ten minutes until regrouping." John nodded, and together they moved deeper into the livestock area, Scout guiding the way. Tonight, the county fair's lights and laughter masked more than merriment—but with Bob and John undercover, no mischief went unnoticed.

Bob and John fanned out along the livestock pens, methodically scanning every shadowed corner. Scout's ears twitched as he sniffed a breeze carrying the scent of sawdust and manure. The dog paused at the edge of a pig pen, head low. Bob crouched beside Scout. "What do you got, boy?" He followed Scout's gaze to a loose plank leaning against the pen—beneath it, a small duffel bag lay hidden. John knelt and unzipped the bag, revealing a stash of stolen wallets, phones, and even a set of car keys. "Jackpot," he murmured, glancing at Bob. "This must be their stash spot." Bob pulled out a pair of gloves and began bagging the items one by one, tagging each piece of evidence. Fairgoers drifted past, unaware of the recovery happening just steps away.

Footsteps approached—Scout's low growl alerted them. A pair of teenagers peeked around the corner, eyes widening at the sight of their loot in police hands. Bob stood and raised his hands. "Evening, folks. Need to explain how these items got here." The teens froze, guilt coloring their faces.

John stepped forward, cuffs in hand. "You're both coming with us." He snapped the cuffs into place with practiced ease. Bob signaled Scout to stand down as he finished securing the last of the evidence. The night's undercover mission had turned up more than a handful of miscreants—it had shut down the entire pickpocket ring operating under the cover of carnival chaos. With all suspects detained, Bob checked his watch. "Time to wrap this up. Meet me back at the Ferris wheel for debrief."

John nodded, guiding the teens past the pens. Scout walked between them, ever watchful, tail high in satisfaction. Bob and John reconvened beside the Ferris wheel's loading platform, the giant wheel's lights casting spinning shadows across the fairground. Scout sat obediently between them, leash slack. John unloaded the last pair of suspects at the patrol wagon. "All picked up?" he asked, checking his notebook.

Bob nodded, patting Scout's harness. "Counted eight wallets, five phones, two sets of car keys, plus overages from the rigged game booth. We shut down the entire ring." John offered Bob a cold bottle of water. "Not bad for a night's work—plus a funnel cake at dawn." Bob took a sip and smiled. "Couldn't have asked for a better partner." He thumbed his radio. "Dispatch, this is Unit 14—undercover op complete. Fairground secure."

"Copy, Unit 14," came Lynn's voice. "Great job." Bob looked up at the Ferris wheel's apex. "Another fair, another story told." He turned to John. "Ready to pack up and call it a night?" John nodded. "First light patrol after we drop off these kids at juvenile hall." He tousled Scout's head. "Then home to Evan." Bob chuckled as they gathered Scout's leash. "Fair's over, but the next adventure's just around the corner." With that, they strode toward the exit—two partners, one K-9, and another chapter closed in the book of Officer Bob's untold stories.

Chapter 13: A Day Off Gone Wrong

Bob slid into the driver's seat of his cruiser early Saturday morning, turning off the usual dispatch alerts. Today was his day off—no cases, no reports, just a quiet day at home. Scout settled in beside him, eager for a different kind of patrol: fetching coffee and errands. He tapped his phone. "Café on Elm, then groceries," he muttered. Scout barked in agreement. Bob eased onto Main Street, enjoying the empty roads and soft sunlight. Fifteen minutes later, he pulled into the café's lot and lifted Scout out. The barista greeted him by name. "Morning, Officer. Usual?" she asked. Bob smiled. "Please." He hooked Scout's leash to the bike rack outside and stepped in, the aroma of espresso warm against the cool morning air. As he waited for his latte, his radio buzzed unexpectedly:

> "Unit 14, we need you—domestic disturbance, Maple Street."

Bob's shoulders tensed. He glanced around—day off or not, duty called. Scout's ears perked. Bob checked the line: "Unit 14 en route." He grabbed his coffee and slipped it into the cruiser's cupholder. Behind him, the barista called, "Stay safe out there!"

Bob nodded, speeding toward Maple Street. Scout sat alert, ready for the unexpected—another untold story beginning before his morning coffee could cool. Bob's cruiser rocketed down Maple Street, lights flashing though no siren sounded—he didn't want to alarm the neighbors more than necessary. Scout sat forward, ears pricked.

He rounded the corner to a small duplex with its front door wide open. Inside, muffled shouting erupted. Bob killed the engine, snapped his radio off "day off" mode, and drew his sidearm, holstering it again after a moment's pause. He stepped onto the porch and called in a calm, firm voice: "Maple Street—Officer Bob. Police!" The yelling stopped. A tense silence hung inside before a woman's voice whispered, "He's drunk again…" Bob eased through the doorway, Scout at his side. In the living room, a man in rumpled pajamas leaned against a coffee table, arms raised defensively. Across the room, his partner cradled a toddler in her arms, tears glinting in the morning light. "Sir, step away from her," Bob instructed, hands open and visible. The man glared but backed off, hands shaking. Bob turned to the woman and child, kneeling to meet their eyes. "Are you okay? Is anyone hurt?" She shook her head, voice trembling: "He smashed the TV remote… but we're fine."

The toddler clutched a stuffed bear. Scout nosed the child gently, earning a small, grateful smile. Bob glanced at the man. "I need your name and date of birth." After securing identification and ensuring the woman and child were safe on the couch, Bob radioed dispatch: "Domestic disturbance—no visible injuries, but I'm separating the parties. Unit 18, can you respond for back-up?"

Outside, the sun climbed higher while Bob managed the scene—day off forgotten in service to the family's safety. John's cruiser pulled up in the driveway just as Bob secured the couple's IDs and checked scene safety. John hopped out, carrying baby Evan in his carrier. "Got your backup," John said quietly, setting Evan on the porch swing under his spouse's watchful eye. "How's it look?" Bob nodded. "No injuries reported. He's volatile but cooperative now. I'm going to separate them until the paperwork's done." He guided the husband into the kitchen and offered water. "I'll need you to sit here while I finish my report." John gave his brother a meaningful glance. "Need a hand with statements?" Bob exhaled. "That'd help. Can you take hers inside? Offer more coffee. Meanwhile, I'll sort his side." John carried the wife and toddler to the living room, handing her a fresh blanket. "I'm Officer John. Your names for the report?"

She managed a small smile through tears. "Maria Santos, and this is Alex." The toddler, still clutching the bear, waved shyly. John listened as Maria recounted the argument—no violence beyond broken electronics—and jotted notes. Scout settled beside the child, keeping watch. In the kitchen, Bob and the husband—Alex—spoke quietly. Alex's voice cracked as he admitted regret. Bob drew up the minimal-disturbance citation and explained options: counseling referral, potential trespass order. Alex nodded, accepting a copy. "I'll get help," he promised.

Back in the living room, John wrapped up Maria's statement. He stepped outside, handing Bob the forms. "We're clear to file," he said. Bob tapped his pen. "Thanks. I'll take them to the station for processing." He radioed dispatch: "Unit 14 and 18—domestic disturbance cleared. Suspect in custody for disorderly conduct. Kid and spouse safe." As they escorted Alex to John's cruiser, Evan cooed from the porch. Bob glanced back at the toddler's bright eyes—reminded how even off-duty, life rarely lets you rest. John glanced down at Evan. "Come on, buddy—time to go home." He moved to buckle the baby in. Bob watched Scout pad beside the cruiser, then turned and inhaled the cool morning air. His day off was gone—but he'd protected a family when they needed him most.

With Alex secured in Unit 18, John gave his brother a nod. "I'll take him in. Are you good here?" Bob wiped sweat from his brow and leaned against the porch railing. "Thanks, John. I'll stay with Maria and the little one until the social worker arrives." John loaded Alex into the back seat and checked his seatbelt before climbing in. He glanced at Evan strapped into his carrier. "Evan's first ride-along—hope he likes the sirens." Bob watched John's cruiser pull away, Scout resting at his feet. He turned back to Maria, offering her a bottle of water. "I called Community Services. They're on their way to check in and help set up counseling." Maria exhaled, relief flooding her features. She hugged the toddler close. "Thank you, Officer Bob. I don't know what we would've done without you." He knelt beside them. "Just doing my job. You two stay safe—help is coming." Scout nudged Bob's hand, reminding him it was time to leave. Bob straightened and checked his watch. It was just past noon—long past the quiet morning he'd planned.

He clipped Scout's leash on and led him toward the cruiser. "Let's get some coffee," Bob said with a gentle laugh. "Guess this day off calls for an overtime latte." Scout barked in agreement as they walked to the car, ready for whatever came next in another day of untold stories.

Bob slid into the driver's seat, Scout's fur warm against his side. He started the engine and pulled back onto Maple Street, the scent of coffee shops mingling with the afternoon air. "Scout, coffee first," he murmured, following the aroma to a café on the corner. He parked, grabbed Scout's leash, and walked inside. The barista, recognizing him from earlier, handed over a fresh latte. Bob tipped her a grateful nod and returned to the cruiser.

As he sipped, his radio crackled:

> "Unit 18 to Unit 14—suspect dropped off. All clear on my end."

Bob tapped his mic: "Copy that, John. Enjoy the rest of your day, brother." He finished his latte, closed the cup lid, and set it in the holder. Scout settled back in for the ride home. The day off hadn't gone as planned, but Bob knew every call—even on his own time—was worth answering.

He glanced at Scout, who rested his head on the dashboard. "Another story told," Bob smiled, pulling away toward home. Bob pulled into his driveway just as a gentle breeze rustled the maples lining the street. Scout hopped down, stretching after the ride. Bob unbuckled his seatbelt and stepped onto the porch, latte in hand.

He opened the door to the warm embrace of home. Sarah looked up from folding laundry. "Rough day?" she asked, handing him a clean towel.

Bob set Scout's leash by the door. "You could say that. Day off turned into a rescue op." He peeled off his jacket and offered the latte. "Thought you might want this." Sarah accepted it with a smile. "You always know when I need coffee." She tousled Scout's ears. "He came in muddy." Scout padded in, tongue lolling, as Bob rinsed his boots. He leaned against the counter. "Managed to keep a family safe, though. And John picked up the slack." Sarah set down her folding. "I saw him earlier with Evan?"

Bob nodded. "Family's doing well. Today reminded me that this job never truly pauses." He watched Scout circle and settled into his bed. "Maybe tomorrow we will take that fishing trip," Sarah teased. Bob smiled, warmth spreading through him. "Promise we'll try—after I submit one more report." He filled Scout's water bowl then poured two mugs of tea. As they settled on the couch, Bob reflected on the unexpected calls that chased him even on his day off—and the comfort of home waiting at the end.

The next morning, sunlight filtered through the blinds as Bob reviewed his tablet—five reports drafted, dozens of incident logs updated. Scout stretched on the floor beside him, tail thumping against the rug. Bob sipped his coffee and tapped the screen: "Submit." He glanced at the clock—still early. At last, a true day off without calls looming. He set down the mug and reached for his hiking boots. "Ready for that fishing trip?" he asked Scout, who barked in agreement.

Outside, the world was calm—no radios crackling, no flashing lights. Bob clipped on Scout's leash and swung open the door. The morning air was crisp, filled with birdsong and promise. He walked down the driveway, Scout leading the way, toward a day unwritten—proof that sometimes, even the busiest officers find a moment to breathe before the next untold story begins. Bob and Scout reached the end of their driveway, where Sarah's car was packed with fishing gear. Bob lifted a tackle box and handed it to Scout's carrier strap—Scout knew this routine well and sniffed the box with anticipation.

Sarah appeared, wearing a wide-brimmed hat and carrying a picnic basket. "Ready?" she called. Bob smiled and took her hand. "Absolutely." He led the way to the car, Scout bounding beside them.

They drove down winding country roads toward Silver Lake, the landscape unfolding in rolling fields and distant tree lines. Scout gazed out the window, ears flapping in the breeze.

Arriving at the boat launch, Bob unloaded the gear. The lake's surface shimmered in the midday sun, undisturbed and inviting. For the first time in days, Bob felt the tension drain from his shoulders.

He and Sarah pushed the small rowboat into the water, Scout balanced between them on the bow. Bob settled into the stern, oars in hand. "All right, partner," he said, scratching Scout behind the ears. "Let's find some fish." Scout let out a happy bark as the boat glided into the center of the lake, the gentle lapping of water against wood the only sound. Bob took a deep breath, savoring the rare peace.

Sunlight danced across Silver Lake as Bob cast his line, the lure skipping twice before settling. Sarah sat beside him, humming softly, while Scout lay stretched out, head resting on his paws.

Bob felt the rod tip jerk. "Got one!" he exclaimed, reeling in with practiced ease. A small bass broke the surface, glinting in the light. He carefully unhooked it and dropped it into the livewell. Sarah clapped. "Nice catch!" Bob smiled, settling back as he recast. The rhythmic motion—cast, wait, reel—felt almost meditative. Scout lifted his head, watching the bobber with interest. After a few quiet moments, Sarah pointed. "Look—oars in the distance." Bob peered toward the far shore and saw two fishermen in a canoe, waving as they drifted by.

Bob waved back. "Good morning to you!" he called. The pair returned the greeting, then continued their leisurely drift. Bob glanced at his watch. "Hard to believe yesterday was chaos." He shook his head, smiling at how quickly life swung between extremes. Scout stood, seeking attention. Bob patted his side. "Go on, buddy," he said. Scout padded to the edge and peered down, sniffing at ripples. A sudden gust sent ripples across the water. Bob caught the lure's flash in the sun and tugged—another bass. He laughed softly, lifting the rod. "Seems like you're hungry today too." The three sat in companionable silence: officer, partner, and family—finding respite on the water before the next story called them back to shore.

The sun dipped low as Bob reeled in his final line. The livewell gurgled softly, housing their day's catch—enough for a hearty dinner. He set the rod aside and stretched, muscles relaxed for the first time in days. Sarah stood and gathered the rods. "Ready to head in?" she asked, brushing stray hair from her face. Scout rose, padding over to Bob and nudging his hand.

Bob scooped Scout into his arms. "Let's go home—to today's dinner and tomorrow's calls." He offered Sarah his free hand. She took it, lacing fingers as they pushed the boat back toward the dock. On the shore, twilight settled in purple hues. Bob paused, looking back at the glassy lake. For a moment, the frantic pace of his duties felt miles away, replaced by gentle waves and the steady breathing of those he loved. He smiled at Scout, then at Sarah. "Another day off…another story told."

Chapter 14: A Letter to the Badge

Bob sat at his desk late that night, the station empty except for the gentle hum of the computers. He opened his leather notebook to a blank page he'd reserved for "Letters to the Badge." Uncapping his pen, he began to write.

> **Dear Badge,**
> Tonight I rested easy knowing our community is safer—dispatch channels clear, families reunited, pickpockets unmasked. You've guided me through every shadow and surprise.

He paused, glancing at the small silver badge pinned to his uniform display case. It caught the overhead light, reflecting a determined gleam back at him. Scout lay curled at his feet, tail flicking in sleep.

Bob continued:

> **You've been my constant companion**
> when the road ran dark and the calls were endless. Through smoke-filled rooms and flooded streets, you reminded me of purpose and promise.

He re-read the words, nodded, then added:

> **I write these letters** not as routine, but as a vow: to honor every story told and every life protected under your watch.

He snapped the notebook closed and tapped the badge display. Outside, the night air was still. Bob stood, slipping the notebook into his jacket pocket. "Another story told," he whispered—and with that, he turned off the desk lamp, ready for the chapters yet to come. Bob sank back into his chair, uncorking a fresh page for the next letter. He wrote:

> **Dear Badge,**
> Tomorrow I'll face new challenges—cases that demand patience, courage, and compassion. But tonight, I'm reminded that every scar and every triumph is etched into your metal.

He paused to sip his coffee, glancing at Scout's peaceful form. The dog's steady breathing felt like a heartbeat echoing through the quiet station. With resolve, Bob added:

> **Thank you** for standing as my
> compass when the path is unclear, and
> for anchoring my commitment to serve.
> With every sunrise, I'm honored to
> wear you.

He tucked the notebook away, placed his pen beside the badge display, and whispered into the empty room, "Until the next story, my friend." Before closing his notebook, Bob paused at the cluster of commendations on his desk—certificates for valor, lifesaving awards, and letters of thanks from community members. He reached for a blank page and began:

> **Dear Badge,**
> Tonight I reflected on the faces behind the calls—the frightened parent, the exhausted rookie, the runaway llama's wide eyes. You gave me the strength to meet each with steady hands and an open heart.

He set down his pen and allowed the weight of the words to settle. Scout stirred, lifting his head. Bob scratched behind his ears.

Picking up the pen again, he added:

> **May I always uphold your promise** to protect and serve, to walk the thin line between order and chaos with honor and humility.

He borrowed one last look at the badge's gleam, then stood, leaving the notebook open—ready for the chapters still unwritten.

Bob rose and walked to the display case where his badge rested on a velvet cushion. He ran his fingers along its edge before writing on the next blank page:

> **Dear Badge,**
> In moments of doubt—when the sirens wail and the road splits into uncertainty—your presence reminds me of why I chose this path. You are more than metal; you are a promise.

He paused to reflect, then beneath his chair the soft click of Scout's tag reminded him of loyalty.

> **Thank you** for standing vigil beside me, for carrying the weight of countless stories, and for shining even in the darkest hours.

Bob closed the notebook and placed it in his top drawer. Turning off the desk lamp, he patted Scout and whispered, "Rest well, partner. Tomorrow is another page."

The next morning, sunlight filtered through the blinds as Bob retrieved his notebook from the top drawer. Scout padded in, nosing the desk in anticipation of a morning routine. Bob flipped to the page marked "Complete" and opened a fresh spread. He began:

> **Dear Badge,**
> Today I will wear you into court, into neighborhoods, and onto streets both familiar and new. May I honor the trust each community places in your symbol.

He closed the notebook and clipped it to his belt. As he left the station with Scout, he felt the weight of the badge's promise steady his steps—ready for the day's calls and the story yet to unfold. During mid-day patrol, Bob helped a nervous first-time voter locate their polling station. As he guided them through the crowd, he thought of his notebook.

Dear Badge,
Today I helped a citizen exercise their voice. Though I wear a uniform, it is their trust and participation that give our democracy strength.

He squeezed the badge over his heart in silent gratitude, knowing each small act was part of a larger commitment to serve and empower. That afternoon, Bob assisted with a school safety drill, standing beside Scout as children practiced lockdown procedures. Reflecting later, he wrote:

Dear Badge,
Among the laughter and questions of eager children, I found hope. You remind me that protection includes preparation, and that our future rests in these young hearts.

He closed the notebook with a quiet smile, the badge gleaming as he led Scout off to the next call. On his lunch break, Bob visited Mrs. Caldwell—the elderly neighbor whose llama ran amok. He brought flowers and news of the zoo's new fence.

Dear Badge,
Today I delivered reassurance: that safety can be restored, and that even the wildest surprises have happy endings under your watch.

He handed Mrs. Caldwell the blooms, feeling the badge's promise bloom anew in her grateful smile. Returning to the station, Bob found a rookie with a trembling voice requesting advice on their first traffic stop. He guided them through the approach, then added to his journal:

Dear Badge,
Mentoring the next generation is as vital as any call. May I always wield your symbol to teach with integrity and compassion.

Scout nosed the rookie's pocket comfortingly, and Bob felt the badge's weight become lighter under shared burden. As dusk fell, Bob and Scout walked the beat along Main Street. Neon signs flickered to life, and shopkeepers locked their doors. He paused beneath a streetlamp and penned his final letter for tonight:

Dear Badge,
 Through every chapter—standoff, rescue, mentorship, or quiet patrol—you and I have carried countless stories. May each verse remain true to the oath we swore.

He snapped the notebook shut and clipped it back in his belt. Scout sat obediently as Bob whispered to the lamp-lit street, "Another story told." Together, they headed home—badge and bearers ready for whatever tomorrow would bring.

Chapter 15: The Final Ride

A soft dawn mist curled along the quiet boulevard as Bob slid into his cruiser, Scout resting in the passenger seat. Today wasn't a call—it was his last scheduled patrol before retirement. He inhaled deeply, tasting the crisp morning air through the open window. John greeted him at roll call, his partner's uniform impeccable. "Ready for your final ride, Bob?" he asked, holding baby Evan asleep in a car seat. Bob smiled, nodding. "Wouldn't miss it for the world." He patted Scout's flank. "Ready, partner?" Scout barked softly, tail thumping. Bob eased the cruiser onto the road, the sunrise painting the sky in gold. Each block they passed felt layered with memories—every corner a story, every streetlamp a witness to untold adventures.

Bob steered the cruiser toward the riverfront district, the skyline's reflection dancing on the water below. John rode shotgun, gently rocking Evan in his arms to keep him asleep. Scout lay quietly, sensing the day's significance. As they passed the old water treatment plant, John nodded. "Remember when you and I busted that jammer there? Feels like a lifetime ago." Bob chuckled softly. "Hard to believe that was only six months back." He flicked on the overhead lights briefly—a silent salute to the tower's silhouette on the horizon.

They turned onto Cedar Creek Road, where floodlights still marked the spot of Bob's midnight rescue. Bob slowed the cruiser, pointing out the reinforced levee. "We kept a family safe here. One of my proudest calls." John smiled down at Evan, who stirred but stayed asleep. "And Scout saved Max in the woods. This city's better because of you, Bob." Bob exhaled, eyes misting. "Couldn't have done it without you, brother." They exchanged a look that spoke volumes, then eased past the creek and onto the tree-lined street leading back downtown—each mile a treasured memory on Bob's final patrol.

They rolled past the site of the empty-house standoff, now a neatly repainted façade with a commemorative plaque tucked beside the front lawn. Bob pointed it out to John. "This is where it all changed—my first big test under fire." John glanced at the building and nodded. "You walked through that door with nothing but steady nerves and your badge. That's the moment you became Officer Bob." Evan cooed softly in his arms, as if in agreement.

Bob's gaze lingered on the plaque:

> *"In honor of Officer Bob's courage, June 4, 1998."*

He tapped the glass of his window. "Feels like yesterday." Scout lifted his head and gave a soft woof, tail wagging in recognition. They continued on, the city waking up around them—shopkeepers opening doors, joggers waving as they passed. Each familiar landmark was a chapter in Bob's career, and today they read together one last time.

Bob guided the cruiser into the precinct's parking area as the morning shift changed over. Uniformed officers tipped their caps, and dispatchers paused to offer him nods of respect. John parked beside him.

Bob killed the engine and sighed, the weight of anticipation settling in his chest. Scout hopped down and stretched. Bob unbuckled his seatbelt and stepped out, running a hand over the cruiser's hood—his faithful companion for so many years. John leaned in, voice soft: "One more stop—let's head inside." They headed toward the front doors together, Scout padding between them. Inside the foyer, a small crowd of colleagues and city officials gathered—coffee cups in hand, smiles and teary eyes blending in the early light. Lieutenant Ramirez stepped forward, extending a hand.

"Bob," she said, voice catching, "it's an honor to have you back one last time." She gestured down the hallway, where a framed photograph of Bob and Scout—taken during the llama rescue—hung among department landmarks. Bob nodded, swallowing. "Thank you, ma'am." He patted Scout's head. "Ready for the send-off, buddy?" Scout let out a happy bark. John clapped Bob on the shoulder. "Let's do this." Together, they moved into the heart of the department, where one final chapter awaited.

In the station's assembly room, rows of chairs were filled with fellow officers, dispatchers, and community leaders. A podium stood at the front, draped with the department's banner. Bob, flanked by John and Scout, approached to warm applause.

Lieutenant Ramirez stepped up to the mic. "Officer Bob, today we honor your 27 years of service, countless rescues, and unwavering dedication." She handed him a folded flag and a commemorative plaque. "On behalf of the city, thank you." Bob accepted them with humility, Scout sitting alert at his side. His voice trembled only slightly as he addressed the crowd:

"This badge has carried me through fires, floods, and every untold story in between. But it's the trust of my partners, my family, and this community that has made me who I am."

He glanced at John—baby Evan in his arms—and then to Scout. "Thank you for walking every mile beside me." The crowd rose, the room filled with standing ovation. Bob's eyes glistened as he folded the flag. Scout nuzzled his hand, and John handed him a quiet salute with Evan's tiny fist mimicking. As applause echoed, Bob realized this wasn't an ending but another chapter's beginning—for him, for John, and for Scout—ready to pass the torch and write new stories. After the ceremony, Bob and John stepped outside into the crisp morning air. Scouts padded at their feet as colleagues lined the walkway, offering congratulations and handshakes.

John handed Bob a set of keys. "Your cruiser—you never want to take her out for a spin again." Bob grinned, taking the keys gently. "One last ride, right?" He glanced down at Scout. "Let's roll, partner." They climbed into the cruiser—Bob in the driver's seat, John riding shotgun with Evan. Scout hopped in behind Bob, tail wagging. With the engine's familiar growl, Bob guided the cruiser out of the parking lot one final time, headlights cutting through the dawn. Bob steered toward the riverfront, the place where his journey had come full circle. As they passed the water's edge, John pointed to a bench beneath the willow trees. "Remember when we first took Scout there after he joined the unit?" John said, smiling down at Evan, who cooed in his arms. Bob nodded. "Best training ground—and quietest office." He parked near the bench, and they all disembarked. Bob unclipped Scout's leash, letting him wander happily in the dewy grass.

They sat, Bob on one side of the bench, John on the other with Evan swaddled in his arms. The river's gentle flow mirrored the steady march of time. Bob closed his eyes for a moment, breathing in the peace. Then he turned to his brother. "Thanks for sharing this ride." John offered Evan to Bob, who cradled his nephew carefully. The baby's eyes met Bob's, and he let out a soft gurgle. Bob laughed quietly. "He's got your eyes, John." He bounced Evan gently. "Little man's ready for his first ride."

John rested his hand on Bob's shoulder. "We've got the next generation covered." He looked at Scout sniffing the shoreline. "And him too." Bob rocked Evan as the sun climbed higher. "Not bad for a final assignment—family, water, and my best partners."

After a few more minutes, Bob stood and stretched. He handed Evan back to John and clipped Scout's leash on again. "Ready to head back?" he asked. John nodded, and they climbed into the cruiser one last time. Bob started the engine, the vehicle's purr a comforting echo. He steered toward home, reflecting on decades of patrols—from gunfights and kidnappings to llamas and lost dogs—and how each story led to this serene morning drive with family at his side.

Pulling into the driveway of John's bungalow, Bob killed the engine. Scout hopped down eagerly, and John lifted Evan out of his carrier. Bob reached into his pocket and retrieved his badge, placing it gently in John's hand. "For safekeeping—until he can wear one." He smiled at Evan. John's eyes misted. "Thanks, Bob." He tucked the badge into a shadow box on the mantel that held photos of Bob, Scout, and their adventures. Bob gathered Scout's leash and ruffled Evan's hair. "Time to close the book on this chapter," he said softly. As the sun peeked over the horizon, Bob Parker—Officer Bob—stepped out of the cruiser one final time. Scout at his side and family before him, he whispered, "Another story told."

Epilogue: A Final Letter & Where Are They Now?

Dear Badge,

Tonight, as these pages close, I write one last time: you have carried me through every unknown turn, every untold story. Now, it's time to pass your promise forward.

Where Are They Now?

- **Officer John & Evan:** In the Parker Community Center's new "Scout's Corner," John teaches three-year-old Evan to tie Scout's retired harness. Laughter echoes as Evan's little fingers fumble with the buckles—another generation learning duty and care.

  You stood for courage when first I faced a darkened closet, for compassion when I cradled a terrified toddler, and for resolve when chaos reigned

- **Officer Chad:** Now Sergeant Chad, he leads the Rookie Ride-Along Program Bob inaugurated. He laces up his boots to guide a fresh recruit—just as Bob did for him—shaping new officers with the same steady hand.

Your metal gleamed in every floodlight rescue and under every Ferris-wheel glow. Your weight reminded me of every life held in trust.

- **Officer Lynn & Dispatch Team:** Lynn heads an annual "Jam-Prevention Workshop," teaching technicians and officers how to safeguard our airwaves. Their motto: "Clear channels save lives," a lesson born from that night at the water-treatment tower.

In every echo—the crackle of a radio, the whistle of floodwaters, the bark of a K-9 partner—you guided me toward hope

- **Ret. Det. Frank Harris:** Each October, he lays flowers beneath the Elmcrest Bridge plaque, honoring Jane Miller with a quiet vigil. He still carries the enhanced photo in his wallet—a reminder that cold cases can, at last, find light.

You bore witness to Lenny's bounding escape and Max's frightened bark—proof that protection wears many faces.

- **Mrs. Caldwell & Lenny the Llama:** Every spring, the Green Valley Petting Zoo hosts "Llama Day," proceeds funding local youth programs. Lenny, fleece freshly trimmed, welcomes children—now a gentle ambassador of community joy.

With you on my chest, I learned that service means more than enforcing rules—it means building bonds, sharing laughter, and offering comfort.

- **Community Center & Flood Drills:** Each September, Cedar Rapids students don safety vests and follow the "Parker Protocol," tracing flood-drill routes Bob designed. Volunteers move sandbags in perfect chains—a legacy of unity engraved in each heart.

So here's my final vow: May every officer who pins on you feel the same call to courage, compassion, and community that guided my steps. May they write new stories in your shine.

Bob snapped the notebook shut and placed it atop his badge display. Scout at his side, John and Evan at his door—together they watched the sunset. Another book concluded, another promise secured.

Thank you, Badge—another story told.

A Note to the Reader
The Untold Stories of Officer Bob
This book wasn't supposed to be mine to finish. It was supposed to be his. My dad started this story with nothing but a blank page, a character named Officer Bob, and a spark of something only he could see. He was supposed to be the one filling these pages with life. He was supposed to be the one deciding how it ended. But life doesn't always wait for the last page. After he passed, the idea of picking this up felt unbearable. I tried and failed. Over and over again. Every time I opened it, the grief came pouring back. Every blank space was a reminder of everything that was missing. Every word I tried to write felt like stealing something sacred that wasn't mine to finish.There were nights where I'd sit there, staring down at the page, too broken to move my hand. Nights where the tears hit the paper before the pen ever could. Nights where I wanted to light the whole thing on fire just to make the pain stop. Because the truth is—
 He should be the one writing this. Not me. And I hated that it wasn't him. I hated how much I wanted to hear his voice telling me what happened next.
I hated that finishing this felt less like honoring him sometimes and more like losing him all over again, every time I touched it.

It took me over four years to write this. Four years of grief. Four years of guilt. Four years of second-guessing if I even had the right to finish what he started. But I kept coming back to it.
Not because it got easier. But because something inside me refused to let this story die unfinished—the same way I refused to let go of him. Finishing this wasn't about the words.
It was about the weight.
It was about carrying something for him when he couldn't carry it anymore. It was about choosing, over and over again, to believe that even broken things are still worth completing.Officer Bob is fictional.But the ache behind him is real. The love behind him is real. And every page of this book carries a little piece of the goodbye I never got to say. Thank you for reading this. Thank you for letting me share a story that mattered long before the first word was ever written. Thank you for being a part of something bigger than just a book.
This isn't just about untold stories. It's about the parts of us we fight to keep alive when the world tries to take them away. It's about writing through heartbreak. It's about finishing what love started—even when it shatters you in the process.
Wherever he is, I hope he knows— We did it. We finished it. And we finished it together. This book is his. It always was. It always will be.
— Evan Lipscomb

Acknowledgments

This book... it's not just a book. It's a piece of someone I lost. And a part of myself I wasn't sure I'd ever be able to reach again. It started with my dad—his ideas, his imagination, his voice on a page that never got the chance to become a full story. But even in those few pages, I saw him. His humor. His heart. His spark. And somewhere in all of it... I felt him asking me to keep going. So I did. To my family: thank you for being patient with me while I carried this. For understanding that grief looks different when it's wrapped in creativity. For reminding me that finishing this wasn't just about the story—it was about healing, too. To my friends: thank you for holding space when I couldn't find the words. For encouraging me when I second-guessed myself. For letting me talk about a fictional character like he was family—because in a strange way, he was. To anyone reading this who's lost someone and still feels their voice echoing in the quiet moments—you're not alone. This book became my way of reaching back through time to hold onto a piece of him. I hope it inspires you to find your own way, too. And to my dad—
 Thank you for giving me the beginning. Thank you for trusting me, even in silence, to find the ending.
 Thank you for showing me that love doesn't disappear. It just finds new ways to show up. This one's for you.

On every page. In every pause. In every part of me that still misses you, every single day.

— Evan

About the Author

Evan Lipscomb didn't expect to write this book. Not like this. Not without the person who started it. But sometimes stories find you again—years later, softer, heavier, and somehow more important than ever. Evan is a writer, actor, and filmmaker who's always used storytelling to make sense of the world. Whether he's in front of the camera or behind the page, his work comes from a place of heart—real, honest, and often shaped by the people who've come and gone from his life. *The Untold Stories of Officer Bob* is more than a story. It's a way to hold onto someone. A way to say goodbye. A way to say, "I remember." This isn't just about a fictional officer. It's about finishing something that matters. It's about honoring the spark his dad left behind. And it's about finding connection—even in silence. When he's not writing, Evan is usually chasing creative sparks, exploring what's next, or quietly reflecting on everything that got him here.
This book may have started with someone else's voice. But the heart behind it is his. And it always will be

This one's for you, Dad. Thank you for every story.

www.ingramcontent.com/pod-product-compliance
Lightning Source LLC
Chambersburg PA
CBHW052030030426
42337CB00027B/4934